Hussar Rocca

Hussar Rocca

A Napoleonic French Cavalry Officer's
Experiences and View of the War Against
the Spanish, British and Guerilla Armies
During the Penninsular Campaign

Albert Jean Michel
de Rocca

LEONAUR

Hussar Rocca: A Napoleonic French Cavalry Officer's Experiences and View of the War Against the Spanish, British and Guerilla Armies During the Penninsular Campaign

by Albert Jean Michel de Rocca

Published by Leonaur Ltd

FIRST EDITION

This version of the text copyright © 2006 Leonaur Ltd

ISBN (10 digit): 1-84677-094-7 (hardcover)
ISBN (13 digit): 978-1-84677-094-4 (hardcover)

ISBN (10 digit): 1-84677-084-X (softcover)
ISBN (13 digit): 978-1-84677-084-5 (softcover)

http://www.leonaur.com

Publisher's Notes

Contents

Publisher's Note

Hussar Rocca is one of the more unusual Napoleonic memoirs in that it gives us a rare insight into an aspect of the Peninsular War not often written about by English—or indeed French—memoirists.

When Napoleon's army invaded the Iberian Peninsula it had not only to contend with the regular armies of Spain, Portugal and England, but with the implacable hatred of the Spanish and Portuguese peoples.

In defence of their countries, humble peasants, farmers, villagers and townsfolk, unaccustomed to fighting and ignorant of the strategy and tactics of the military, mobilised into powerful and effective guerrilla armies, which took the fight to the French in the mountains and hills. Here, knowledge of the terrain and what might be termed "indiscipline" were huge advantages. The French were unaccustomed to this kind of warfare and certainly had no workable means of counteracting the guerillas.

These peoples' armies attacked and harried the French, slaughtering many without mercy; raided their supply trains, so successfully that the invaders were often on the point of starvation, and destroyed their lines of communication. They also pursued a "burnt earth" policy, often at great cost to themselves, to ensure that neither food, wine, animals or other supplies were left for the French to use in furthering their conquest and subjugation of the Spanish people.

Although written from a French perspective, this is a story of great national bravery on the part of the Spanish and Portuguese peoples, and, despite his notional enmity, Rocca's admiration and warmth for them shines through on almost every page—even when he is their victim!

For this edition the Leonaur editors have revisited the text and substantially rewritten parts of it to make it less ambiguous and muddled. What was a clumsy, frequently misleading and sometimes incorrect translation, is now, we feel, both more readable and more consistent. Of the events Rocca describes, none have been changed in terms of either their factual content or the importance Rocca places on them; we have remained true to the spirit of Rocca's words. The result of our work is, we think, possibly the most accessible edition of this important book there has yet been. We hope you agree with us!

The Leonaur Editors

Chapter 1

FROM GERMANY TO SPAIN

In 1808, the year after the close of the campaign which terminated with the battle of Friedland and the peace of Tilsit, the 2nd Regiment of Hussars, formerly named Chamboran, in which I had the honour to serve, received orders to leave Prussia, and march for Spain. I thus had an opportunity afforded me to compare two very different kinds of military service—the war of regular troops, who seldom concern themselves with the reasons why they are at war, and, by way of contrast, the resistance of a nation, fighting for existence against a disciplined conquering force.

My regiment was finally leaving the sandy plains of northern Germany, where we had been engaged with a people almost universally subject to military despotism. The princes of the Germanic empire had, for more than a century, turned all their attention to the perfection of the military system, in order to establish their authority, and promote their personal ambition. But, in training their vassals to absolute obedience, they had weakened the national character—the main rampart against foreign invasion, the only invincible bulwark of national strength.

When a province of Germany was conquered by the French, and could no longer obey its sovereign's commands, the lower classes, unaccustomed to acting of their own volition, dared not move a step without the orders of their lords or their governments. The conquered governments became subject to their conqueror's demands; and their lords, well aware of the constant vexations which the people experienced from the invading army, were compelled to accept the evils which war introduces.

In Prussia, the clergy did not dominate the people. Among Protestants, the Reformation had removed that dominion which the priests still maintain in some Catholic countries—above all, in Spain. Learned men, who might have influenced public opinion, and put their knowledge and abilities at the service of of their country, were rarely called upon to take part in public affairs. And thus it appeared that the sole aim of their ambition was literary renown and the respect of their equals; they saw no reason to apply themselves to those pursuits and studies which were essential to the circumstances of the times. The real authority of many of the States in Germany was based upon their military systems; and their political existence depended on the energy or ineptitude of their governments.

On the plains of Germany, the nature of the countryside did not, as in countries of a more barren, marshy, or mountainous nature, provide means of escape from the yoke of the conquerors. Small bodies of troops were sufficient to control large areas of land, keep it's people subjugated, and to ensure our armies of their necessary supplies. The citizens could have found no secure places of retreat, had they been disposed to any partial revolts; besides, the Germans, being accustomed to a quiet and uniform life, are only provoked to desperate exertions by the complete derangement of their habits.

The war in Germany was wholly carried on between troops of the line, among whom there exists rivalry rather than hatred. From the inhabitants of the conquered Countries we had nothing to fear. The success of a campaign depended on the unity of military operations, the ability and perseverance of the chiefs, their sagacity to foresee and anticipate, and in bringing forward, opportunely and promptly, to decisive points of attack, overpowering masses of troops. We were not exposed to those petty skirmishes, which, in regular warfare, only increase suffering, without contributing to general advantage; and the capacity of generals was never defeated by individual interference, or popular spontaneous movements.

In Germany we had only to conquer governments and armies: in the Spanish Peninsula, where we were now carrying our arms, there no longer existed either the one or the other. The Emperor Napoleon had invaded Portugal and Spain—had put to flight or taken captive the sovereigns of these two countries—and had dispersed their military forces. We had not now to contend with regular troops, everywhere almost the same, but with a people who, in their manners, their prejudices, and the very nature of their country, were isolated from every other nation on the Continent. The Spaniards were determined to oppose us because they believed that Napoleon would make of the Iberian Peninsula, for all of time, a state subject unalterably to the dominion and will of France.

It is a fact that Spain as a society, in terms of its knowledge, and skill in social arts, was more than a century less advanced than other countries of Europe. Its remote and isolated situation, and the power of its ecclesiastical establishments, had deterred the Spaniards from interfering in those disputes and controversies of the sixteenth century, which had enlightened and advanced the rest of Europe. They concerned themselves little with the philosophical spirit of the eighteenth century, to which the French Revolution may in part be ascribed.

However, though the Spaniards were sunk in indolence, and though that confusion and corruption which inevitably follow a long despotism were manifest in their administration, still their national character remained unimpaired. Their government, arbitrary as it was, in no respect resembled the absolute military power of Germany—where the changeless dominance of the ruling princes was so admirably calculated to paralyze the energies of individual character.

It is true, that Ferdinand the Catholic, Charles V. and Philip II., had assumed nearly all the privileges of the Grandees and Cortes, and prostrated the liberty of Spain. But, in spite of the despotism of these sovereigns, their ineptitude of government could not destroy in the people a liberty of action, which often gave rise to insubordination.

In the annals of German monarchies, we read only of princes and armies. In Spain, since the time that Ferdinand the Catholic reunited the different kingdoms into one, there has scarcely been a reign during which the ordinary people have failed to prove their independence of will by defying their monarch or deposing ministers or favourites. When the inhabitants of Madrid rose in insurrection, to demand from Charles III., father of Charles IV., the dismissal of his minister Squilaci, the king himself was constrained to appear, accompanied by a monk holding a crucifix, to appease the people, and to strengthen his influence. The court, which had fled to Aranjuez, then endeavoured to march the Walloon guards against Madrid; but the people, killing several, raised the universal shout..... "*Si entraran los Vallones, no reyneran los Borbones.*"—"If the Walloons enter, the Bourbons shall not reign." The guards did not enter. Squilaci was dismissed, and order was restored.

In Berlin and Prussia, the inhabitants honoured the soldiers of their king in their military capacity, as the soldiers honoured their commanders. In Madrid, the soldiers on duty while executing their sovereign's orders, gave way to the common citizens.

The revenues of the Spanish crown being very limited, few troops could be maintained. With the exception of some privileged companies, the regiments of the line were incomplete, ill paid, and ill disciplined. Ecclesiastics were the only powerful and efficient militia of the Spanish kings. They restrained and dispersed the riots of the populace by the 'artillery' of sermons, and by the 'standards' of pontifical ornaments and relics.

The lofty and sterile mountains which run throughout and around Spain, were inhabited by a warlike, indomitable people who were always armed, to protect themselves whilst carrying on their smuggling activities, and trained to repulse the regular troops of their nation, often sent in pursuit of them.

The people of Spain were almost wholly governed by the clergy. Their priests were hostile to the French, as much from self interest as from patriotism. They knew well that it was intended to deprive them of their privileges, and to deny them their patrimony and patronage. Their concerns and grievances became those of the community at large. Every Spaniard regarded a public grievance as his personal quarrel. So it was that we had about as many foes to fight, as the Peninsula could number inhabitants.

Other obstacles existed to deprive us of the means, as we had in northern Germany, of retaining our conquests and securing our communications and supplies. The mildness of the Spanish climate throughout the year was such as to permit living in the open air, and meant the populace could abandon their houses without any hardship or regret; their mountains afforded them retreats inaccessible to us; and the sea everywhere presented opportunities of escape. Besides, the numerous ships and terrible Navy of England gave the Spanish the means of increasing their strength, whether by transporting them speedily to our vulnerable points, or by giving wings to their flight, and supplying them with a refuge from the pursuit of our victorious troops.

When we broke up our cantonments in Prussia for the purpose of going to Spain, we believed we were marching on an easy expedition, which would be of short duration. Conquerors in Germany, we never once imagined that any thing could resist us. We never reflected on the unforeseen difficulties which the nature of the country so new to us, and the character of the inhabitants, might present.

Our soldiers never inquired whither they were going. If there was food and drink to be had in the country they must visit, it was the only point of view from which they regarded their destination. To our French soldiers the world had but two divisions—the blessed zone where the vine grows, and the miserable region where it is unknown.

Being told, at the commencement of each campaign, that they were called on to strike the last blow at the tottering power of the English, they were ready to confront that power in all its forms. England itself our soldiers judged their distance from by the number of marches they had made. For years, from one end of the world to the other, they had been seeking this remote and visionary country, which remained distant no matter how much they pursued it. At length they said: "if the desert divided us from England in Egypt, and the sea at Boulogne, we shall soon reach it by land in crossing Spain".

The Elbe and the Weser being passed, the 2nd Hussars reached the left bank of the Rhine and France. When we quitted Prussia, in September 1808, the likelihood of a war with Austria had been spoken of for two months, and none of us doubted but our march was towards the Danube. Our troops bade farewell to Germany with heavy hearts, and almost with tears—that lovely land which they had conquered....that country of war, from whence they carried so many memorials of glory, and where, at the same time, they had often known that they had made themselves beloved!

We passed through France as if it had been a country lately conquered and subdued by our arms. The Emperor Napoleon had ordained that his soldiers should be everywhere well received and entertained. Deputations from his faithful cities came to compliment us at their gates. The officers and soldiers were conducted, on their arrival, to splendid feasts prepared for their reception; and on our departure the magistrates thanked us, over and above, that they had been pleased to spend, in one day, the special revenue of many weeks of their municipal funds.

The soldiers of the grand army did not lose the custom in France they had contracted in Germany, of sometimes abusing the citizens and peasants with whom they were quartered. The foreign auxiliary troops, especially, would not be convinced that they ought not to conduct themselves in France as in an enemy's country. They told us it must be the common practice, since the French troops behaved not otherwise among them in Germany and Poland. The inhabitants of the towns and districts where we passed, bore it all with patience, and calmly waited until the armed torrent flowed past.

Our troops were composed (besides French) of Germans, Italians, Poles, Swiss, Dutch, Irish and even Mamelukes from Egypt. These strangers were all clad in the costume of their own countries; they retained their own customs, and spoke their native languages. But notwithstanding the difference of manners which raises barriers between nations, they were easily trained, by military discipline, into a united whole. All these men wore the same cockade, and had but one cry to fight and rally.

We crossed the Seine at Paris, the Loire at Saumur, the Garonne at Bourdeaux. We enjoyed there some days rest, for the first time since we left Prussia, whilst the remainder of the army were reaching the opposite bank of the river. We travelled next through the uncultivated heaths which lie between Bourdeaux and Bayonne. The sandy soil of these solitary plains, like the moors of Prussia and Poland, did not resound under the tread of our horses, or echo back their regular and accelerated pace, to reanimate their ardour.

Vast forests of cork-tree and pine bounded the horizon in the distance; and shepherds, clad in the black skins of their sheep, were observed at wide intervals, mounted on stilts, six or seven feet in height, and supported by long poles. They remained stationary in one place, without ever losing sight of their flocks, which fed on the moors around them. When the Emperor Napoleon crossed these immense heaths, the poverty of the country could not afford the etiquette of a mounted honour guard. His escort was a detachment of these shepherds, who marched foot for foot on their long stilts, with our horses trotting in the sand.

A few leagues beyond Bayonne we arrived at the Bidassoa, a stream which bounds France among the Pyrenees. The moment we set foot on the Spanish territory, an evident difference was perceived in the face of the country, and the manners of the inhabitants. The narrow winding streets of their towns—their grated windows—their doors perpetually shut—the stern and reserved air of all classes of inhabitants—their suspicion of us so very generally manifested; all tended to increase that unnatural sadness which possessed every one of us on our entrance into Spain.

We saw the Emperor Napoleon pass on horseback, before he arrived at Vittoria. He was remarkable, from the simplicity of his green uniform, among the splendid dresses of his generals around him. He waved his hand particularly to each officer as he passed, as if he would have said—"I depend on you." French and Spaniards flocked around him on his way. The former beheld in him alone the fortune of the entire army. The Spaniards were intent to gather, from his aspect and carriage, what fate was awaiting their unhappy country.

About the end of October 1808, the Grand army of Germany formed a junction with the French army under the command of King Joseph in Spain. There, with surprise, we first learned from our brethren in arms, part of the events of the Peninsular war, and the details[*] of those unhappy actions which had compelled Generals Dupont and Junot to capitulate in Andalusia and Portugal, Marshal Moncey to raise the siege of Valencia, and the whole army, in a word, to retire and concentrate itself on the left bank of the Ebro.

---

[*] King Joseph was at Vittoria with the general staff of his army and his guards. Marshal Moncey, with his corps of observation, was at Tafalla, watching the Spanish army of General Palafox, stationed at Sanguessa, on the frontiers of Navarre and Arragon. The troops under the command of Marshal Ney kept possession of Logrono and Guardia. The Spanish armies, commanded by Generals Castanos and Palafox, about 40,000 strong, when united, lay before them in the environs of Tudela on the Ebro. Marshal Bessieres was at Miranda on the Ebro, in a position covered by the numerous and well-mounted cavalry of General Lassalle. In falling back, he had left a garrison in the citadel of Pancorvo. Marshal Lefevre occupied Durango. The troops under Marshal Bessieres and Lefevre faced the centre and the left of the Spanish forces under Generals Belvidere and Blake. The central Spanish army, stationed at Burgos, might not amount to more than 12,000, or 14,000 men. It was to be reinforced by 26,000 English, which were on their march from Portugal and Corunna, under Generals Moore and Sir D. Baird. This army was designed to sustain that of the left, which General Blake commanded in Biscay, and to keep the communication open with the Spanish armies in Arragon and Navarre.

The army of General Blake, although 37,000 strong, had few cavalry, and therefore dared not descend into the flat country around Miranda and Vittoria. It had abandoned its position between Ona Frias and Erron, to occupy Bilbao; and had penetrated through the mountains which separate Biscay from the province of Alva, towards Durango, as far as Zamora and Archandiano, in order to raise the country, cut off the communications, and attack the right of the army of King Joseph. The Spanish armies of Navarre and Arragon were to perform the same movement against the centre and left wing of the French, for the purpose of compelling them to fall back by way of Tolosa, or of forcing them into the defiles of Navarre towards Pampeluna. Such were the designs of the Spaniards, and the situation of affairs, when Napoleon took the command of the armies in that country.

The army of General Blake was attacked on the 31st of October, near Durango, by the corps of Marshal Lefevre. He repulsed it, and entered Bilbao the day following. Marshal Victor s corps, which was to form, along with that of Lefevre, the right of our army, moved on the 6th of November from Vittoria towards Ordunna.

Chapter 2

WAR AGAINST THE SPANISH

During the night of November 8th, the Imperial quarters were removed from Vittoria to Miranda. Next day the whole army of the centre, of which our Hussars formed a part, commenced its march under the command of Napoleon himself. We were to make a determined attempt upon Burgos, where the centre of the Spaniards was stationed; then, by a rapid advance, to menace the flanks of their right and left in Biscay, and the frontiers of Navarre and Arragon. We wished to prevent these troops, if they retired, from concentrating themselves at Madrid; and to destroy their communications, by throwing ourselves on their rear, if they offered any resistance.

To effect this, our army of the right, composed of the troops under Marshals Victor and Lefevre, were to prosecute their march against the army of Blake, who, having been repulsed from Durango and Valmeceda, was now retiring upon Espinosa. Our army of the left, commanded by Marshals Lannes and Moncey, remained in the neighbourhood of Logrono and Tafalla, waiting only for the result of the action, which we confidently expected at Burgos, to ascend the Ebro, and march towards Saragossa.

On the evening of the 9th, the Imperial quarters were taken up at Breviesca. The army, commanded by the Emperor, was cantoned in the neighbourhood of the town.

The inhabitants of the country had all fled to the mountains when we approached. At daybreak of the 10th, Marshal Soult, with a division of infantry, went to reconnoitre the positions of the enemy in the direction of Burgos. On arriving at the village of Garnonal, he was received with a discharge of thirty pieces of cannon. The French regarded this as the signal for attack. Marshal Soult, without waiting for the rest of our army which followed, instantly engaged, and broke the Walloons and Spanish guards, who formed the enemy's principal strength. Marshal Bessieres then arriving with the cavalry, successfully attacked the wings, completed their discomfiture, and entered Burgos with the fleeing fugitives.

Of the whole army, our brigade of Hussars alone was not engaged. Our cantonment was a secluded place, about two leagues from Breviesca. The adjutant, whose duty it was to bring us our orders to march, went astray, for want of a guide; and we only set out at nine in the morning to follow the army. The whole day we pursued the same track, without suspecting what had passed in the forenoon. When night approached, we discerned at a great distance the fires of the advanced guard. Notwithstanding the darkness, we perceived, by the motion of our horses, that we were in the act of passing a field of battle. Every now and then they slackened their pace, and lifted their feet cautiously, as if afraid of doing injury to the inanimate dead who lay below. Sometimes they would stop for a moment, and, bending their heads, would smell with evident terror the carcasses of the horses that had been killed.

Burgos was completely deserted by its inhabitants. That large city was one vast solitude when our troops arrived there after the battle, and it was at once given up to be pillaged. In the quarter where we entered, the confused hum of voices, and the noise of the soldiers going hither and thither, seeking provisions and cooking utensils in the for-saken houses, were heard everywhere around us. For light, they carried in their hands immense waxen tapers, which they had found in the neighbouring convents. In a distant part of the city, less frequented by our soldiers, was heard the hollow, mournful moaning of the sick and aged, who, too feeble for flight, had taken refuge in a church, where they were crowded together in heaps. There, repeating their prayers with their clergy, they awaited the death which they believed approaching. The glass-windows of the church were dimly lighted with sacred lamps. The Spaniards, in the full confidence that they would obtain a great victory over us, had collected immense quantities of wool to take to the south of France. We passed through the enormous packs,—built up like two lofty walls on either side, which they confidently expected to take with them along with the baggage of their troops. It was but one hour to midnight when we arrived at the place where we were appointed to bivouack, on the banks of the Arlanzon. At daybreak we saw, in the shallow river which ran near us, the corpses of some Spanish soldiers and monks, who had been killed in battle the preceding day.

On the 11th, at sunrise, our troop of light cavalry be-gan to explore the country up-stream of the Arlanzon. We discovered at a distance, as we proceeded up the river, bands of the townsmen and peasantry skulking behind the heights, or among the precipices of the opposite banks. Often we perceived their heads from time to time raised above the brushwood, to observe if we were past.

Some of our flankers fell in with a few poor nuns, who had abandoned Burgos during the battle of the previous day. These sisters, some of whom had never been be-yond their own cloisters, had fled in their terror as far as they had strength to go, and had come to hide themselves in the thickets adjoining the river. They were scattered about when they first saw us at a distance; but they ran together on our approach, and kept kneeling close beside each other, muffled in their cloaks, and their heads bent to the ground. One of them, who seemed to possess more courage than the rest, stood up, and placed herself before her companions. Her appearance indicated sincerity and dignity, and the calm stillness of despair. As the soldiers passed before her, while she touched the beads of her rosary, she addressed to them these three words, all she knew of our language, "*Bonjours, Messieurs Français,*" as if claiming their protection. These poor nuns were suffered to remain in peace.

We spent four days in a town about four leagues from Burgos, the name of which I never learned, as we found no person to inquire at. The Imperial quarters continued at Burgos till the 22nd. That town was the centre of all the military operations; and from thence it was easy to hold communications with the different corps in Biscay and Arragon, to attend to their movements, end to reinforce them if required.

The day after the engagement at Burgos, several detachments were sent in pursuit of the enemy, to annihilate an army which one victory had easily dispersed, but could not have entirely destroyed. Ten thousand cavalry, with twenty pieces of light artillery, were despatched with all haste by way of Placencia, Leon, and Zamora, to fall behind the English army, which was believed to be at Valladolid. Marshal Soult placed himself on the rear of the Spanish army of the left, by Villarcayo and Reynosa. A division of infantry proceeded by a near route, to take possession of the passes of the mountains of Saint Ander. These troops saw no more of the enemy, notwithstanding the rapidity of their march. Since the affair at Durango, the army of

General Blake had in vain attempted to rally successively at Guenes and Valmeceda. Pursued by Marshal Victor in the direction of Espinosa, by Marshal Lefevre in that of Villarcayo, after two days' hard fighting, it was at last completely overthrown on the 6th of November at Espinosa.

The Spanish armies of the centre and left having now been overcome in every direction, it was only necessary to disperse their right, in order to march upon Madrid. For this purpose, the corps of Marshal Ney was despatched from Burgos, through Lerma and Aranda, with instructions first to ascend the Douro, then to descend in the direction of the Ebro, and take Generals Castanos and Palafox in the rear, who were speedily to be attacked in front by our army of the left, under Marshals Lannes and Moncey. This army of the left still occupied Logrono and Tafalla, and were preparing again to descend the Ebro.

On the 15th of November, our brigade of Hussars proceeded to Lerma to reinforce the army of Marshal Ney, with which it was henceforth to be provisionally attached. On the 16th, Marshal Ney went from Lerma to Aranjuez. The inhabitants, on our approach, uniformly abandoned their houses, and carried with them to the distant mountains their most precious effects. That solitude and desolation which conquering armies usually leave behind them, seemed universally to have preceded us.

In approaching the deserted cities and villages of Castile, we no longer perceived the wreaths of smoke incessantly rising in the air, and forming a second atmosphere above those populous and well inhabited towns. Instead of the continual noise and hum of living beings, no sounds were heard within the walls but the tolling of bells announcing the flight of time, whose progress we could not retard, and the hoarse groaning of the ravens hovering around the elevated spires. The houses, now empty, served for the most part only to reverberate the deep-toned drums, or the shrill trumpets, in heavy echoes of discordancy.

Our lodgings were speedily appointed. Each regiment occupied a quarter, every company a street, according to the size of the town. A few minutes after our arrival, our soldiers were as much at home in their new mansions, as if they had come to colonize the place. This warlike and migratory population would then begin to denominate anew the situations which they occupied. Here was "Dragoon's quarter,"—"Such a company's street,"—"General's house,"—"Main-guard place,"—"Parade square." There, on the walls of a convent, might be seen "Barracks of such a battalion." Again, before the cell of some deserted cloister, a sign would be suspended with this inscription,—"Here is the Prince of Parisian cooks." This personage was a sutler, who had hastened to establish in this place his ambulatory tavern.

When the army arrived at the place where it had to rest, too late to distribute the quarters with regularity, we then lodged *militairement* or promiscuously, and without any order, wherever we found room. As soon as the main guard was stationed, at a well-known signal, the whole army disbanded, running up and down in a burly-burly, like a swollen torrent, through the city; and for half an hour after, nothing was heard but the loud shouts of the soldiers, and the clanking of doors, which they forced open with repeated blows of hatchets or stones. The grenadiers hit upon a plan as speedy as effectual, for gaining admittance where they wished. They held their muskets to the key-holes, and blew away the locks; thus rendering the precautions of the citizens useless, who never forgot to lock their doors when they fled at our approach.

Our army left Aranda on the morning of the 20th, and for two hours we ascended the Douro, without hearing a word of the enemy, or meeting with a human being. On the evening of the 21st, we observed on a sudden some hesitation on the part of our scouts. We instantly formed into squadrons; and soon after the platoon of the advanced guard was engaged with a corps of the enemy, which it easily repulsed. We made some prisoners as we entered Almazan.

The army bivouacked that night under the walls of the town, the inhabitants of which had all fled. It was too late to make the regular distributions; and unhappily, for half an hour, it was impossible to prevent pillage to supply the immediate wants of the troops. The same evening we despatched, in different directions, reconnoitring parties of twenty-five Hussars. The detachment which went in the direction of Siguenza, returned in the nighttime with some prisoners and baggage. The day following, our army took the road to Soria. Our regiment, the 2nd of Hussars, alone remained at Almazan, to keep open the communications with Burgos through Aranda, and to watch the corps of the enemy, which were reported to be around Siguenza, Medina-Coeli, and Agrida.

I received orders at daybreak of the 24th, to go with twenty-five mounted men, and reconnoitre on the road from Almazan to Agrida. Having no guide, I ascended with my troop the right bank of the Douro, according to an incorrect French map, which led me astray. After four hours hard riding among cross-roads, we perceived two children, who fled to the woods uttering screams of terror. I followed them alone, and arrived in the midst of an encampment of females who had fled from the neighbouring villages, with their children and flocks, to take refuge in a little island formed by the river. I came upon them so suddenly, that I had time to assure them by signs of their safety before my detachment came up. I made the interpreter, who accompanied me, inquire which was the direct road from Almazan to Agrida. The only man among them, an aged clergyman, replied, that we were more than four leagues distant, and directed to the proper road on the opposite bank of the river. We passed through a succession of villages and hamlets, inhabited only by men, and came at last to the place we intended.

The person who acted as my interpreter was a Flemish deserter, that had been forced, from hunger and the dread of being murdered by the peasants, to surrender himself after the action at Burgos. We had surnamed him Blanco, because he had wrapped his body in the white habit of a Dominican Friar, which he had got from the Hussars, covering his old and tattered uniform of the Walloon guards, and defending himself from the cold. To crown the whole, he had shielded his head with the huge hat of that religious order. In the inhabited villages we passed through, the people, seeing him marching on foot before us, conceived he was a true monk, whom we had compelled to bear us company. They saluted the reverend father most profoundly, lamented his unhappy fate, and everybody gave him money. Delighted with his honours, he would not abandon his lucrative costume, even when he had it in his power.

We again wandered for want of a guide, and marched for nine hours in a journey of only four leagues. The difficulty of procuring guides was constantly occuring, because we found no inhabitants wherever we went. The same evening our regiment received orders to leave Almazan. We marched a night and a day nearly, without stopping, and rejoined the corps of Marshal Ney, just as he entered Agrida by the road from Soria. The infantry were quartered in the town. The light cavalry were sent to cover the position of the army a league further on, in the road to Cascante. We believed ourselves to be close on the rear of the left wing of the Spanish troops.

The city of Agrida was without a living soul. The commander of our troops could find no guide, and we were obliged once more to use our map in search of the cantonment appointed us. Night came on, and we were not long of losing our way among the passes of the mountains. Deceived by the thick mists in which we were enveloped, we fancied ourselves every moment on the brink of some yawning precipice. Every hundred paces of our march we halted, whilst the foremost of the column explored the path among the rocks, almost groping with their hands. Then, for a long time, in the deep stillness of the night, no sounds were heard but the shiverings of the horses, the heavy tramp of their feet, and the clamping of their bits, in their impatience to be stabled. We had dismounted, and were marching in file, listening and repeating from one to another the warnings of bad steps and precipices—speaking in an under-tone, that we might not give the alarm to a body of troops whose half-extinguished fires we perceived on the far side of the ravine. We knew not whether they were friends or foes; but an attack of infantry, in our present situation, would have been inevitably fatal.

In this manner we passed the most of the night, marching and countermarching continually. A little before daybreak the moon rose, and we found ourselves much about where we were when darkness overtook us. We were at the bottom of a narrow valley, and in sight of the little village where we should have bivouacked. For thirty hours we had been on the march. Thus, the impossibility of obtaining guides, exposed us to a thousand unexpected and unheard of difficulties at every step of our progress. In these thinly peopled districts, where every person was against us, we scarcely found an individual to give us the least account of the enemy, either true or false.

We were apprised, but too late, that the army of Generals Castanos and Palafox had been completely routed at Tudela on the 23rd. If we had arrived one day sooner at Agrida, the dispersed columns of Spaniards who were retreating to Madrid, would have been intercepted by us, and made prisoners in that city.

Our army of the left, whose movement we should have seconded, had concentrated itself on the 22nd at the bridge of Lodosa. On the 23rd, the Spanish army of the right was seen between the villages of Tudela and Cascante, drawn up in order of battle, a full league in extent. Marshal Lannes, with a division of infantry marching in close column, drove in the centre of the enemy's line. General Lefevre's cavalry immediately rushed into the breach, and by a lateral movement, surrounded the right wing of the Spaniards. Broken in one point, they could no longer manœuvre. They retreated in disorder, leaving 30 pieces of cannon, a great number of prisoners, and many dead on the field of battle.

Since the retreat of King Joseph over the Ebro in the month of July, the Spaniards had assumed so mighty a confidence in their own strength, that their concern when they had to contend with us, was not so much how to make the best resistance, or to secure their retreat in case of a reverse, as that none of the French should escape them. They prejudged the event of the combat, by their ardent desire to overcome and annihilate their foes. Unskilled in the science of war, ignorant of manœuvring, and only afraid they could not extend their columns soon enough to surround us; they drew themselves up in long lines of no depth, in plains where our cavalry and superior tactics gave us every advantage. This order of battle, injudicious even for well-disciplined troops, deprived these Spaniards of the ability to support with speed the points threatened by our columns, or of concentrating themselves to resist our solid masses. In Biscay and the Asturias, our troops had received more opposition, because they had there to fight in a mountainous country, where local difficulties and individual courage may sometimes baffle the skill of military science. Before they could reach Reinosa, they had to contend for victory at Durango, Zornosa, Guones, Valmeceda, and last at Espinosa.

At that time not a Frenchman doubted that the fate of Spain would be decided by these rapid victories. We believed, and so did all Europe, that we had only now to march to Madrid, to complete the subjugation of Spain, and the organization of the country *à la maniere Française*; or, in other words, to increase our means of further conquest by all the resources of our vanquished enemies. We had been accustomed to see no force but the military, in the countries where we had hitherto waged war. The spirit which inspired the citizens we counted a mere nothing.

On the 26th of November, Marshal Ney's corps proceeded towards Borja, by way of Cascante. General Maurice Mathieu, with a single division, took the same route a day earlier, and made several prisoners on the march. On the 27th we arrived at Alagon, a small town about four leagues distant from Saragossa, whose numerous spires we discerned at a distance.

The Arragonese, by no means disheartened by the late reverses of fortune, had determined to defend themselves in the city of Saragossa. They had not been able to surround it with regular fortifications, but they had converted every dwelling to a fortress; and every convent, every house, required a separate assault. These kinds of fortifications are of all others perhaps best calculated to prolong a siege.

Palafox, with ten thousand men, whom he had preserved from the battle at Tudela, had thrown himself into the place. These identical soldiers of the army of Arragon, whom we had already vanquished in the open field almost without effort, resisted us, as citizens, within the compass of this principal city, for nearly a whole year.

Fifty thousand peasants rose in arms for the defence of Saragossa. From every quarter they threw themselves into the town, even through the midst of our victorious columns. They had no other fear but of arriving too late, where their hearts and their country called them. "We have been shielded for ages," they said, " by the Virgin de Pillar, mighty in miracles. We flocked in crowds in happier times, making pilgrimages to her shrine, to implore a blessing on our harvests; and shall we now leave her altars defenceless?"

The character of the Spaniards of these provinces has no parallel of resemblance with the other nations of Europe. Patriotism is with them another name for religion, as it was among the ancients, where no people despaired, or confessed themselves subdued, as long as they could preserve the altars of their patron deities unharmed. The sacred ensigns of Jupiter Capitolinus, displayed in battle, led the Romans to victory. After the days of chivalry, when modern armies were again organized like those of Rome, the religious sentiment which bound the Roman soldier to his standard, was compensated among regular troops by the principle of honour. The military point of honour has made the armies disciplined on this principle attain to high excellence. But it is patriotism alone, either religious or political, that can render nations invincible.

The people of Spain were actuated only by religious patriotism. They had no practical knowledge of the discipline, or of the science of war. They soon abandoned

30

their colours when defeated. They did not think themselves bound to maintain their promise to an enemy. But they had only one interest, and one common sentiment— to avenge, by every possible expedient, the injuries their country sustained.

Among others, one of the insurgent peasants of Arragon was seized by our scouts: He was armed only with a musket, and was driving an ass before him, which carried a stock of several months' provisions. The officer who commanded the vanguard pitied the poor fellow, and commanded his deliverance, making signs that he might fly to the mountains. The peasant took the hint; but the moment he was at liberty he loaded his gun, returned to our ranks, and took aim at his deliverer. The ball happily missed. This Spanish peasant hoped to die a martyr, for killing, as he falsely thought, one of our principal leaders. At the halt be was brought before the Colonel of the regiment. Out of curiosity we all surrounded him. One of our Hussars, by a particular action having persuaded him he was to be shot, he instantly fell on his knees, prayed to God and the Virgin Mary, and courageously awaited death. He was raised up, and sent at night to head-quarters. If these men had known how to fight as they knew how to die, we would not have passed the Pyrenees so easily.

Marshal Lannes, with his *corps d' armée*, remained in Arragon to carry on the siege of Saragossa. The force under Marshal Ney continued, by rapid marches, to pursue the broken fragments of Castanos's army, which were retreating towards Guadalaxara and Madrid. Our van-guard, on the 28th, cut to pieces the rear-guard of the Spaniards in attempting to secure the pass of Buvierca on the Xalon.

The forced marches of our army were often prolonged after night-fall; and then, in passing nigh the squadrons of Italians, Germans, and French, we could hear them singing their national airs, to forget their fatigues, and recall, in a distant and hostile land, recollections of their native country.

When the night was far advanced, the army stayed in the environs of deserted towns and villages, and then we found ourselves in want of every thing. But the soldiers were soon spread over every quarter to forage, and in less than an hour they had transferred what yet remained in the houses of the neighbourhood to their bivouack. Around large fires, lighted at intervals, were then to be seen all the apparatus of military cookery. On one side, some were constructing barracks in great expedition, with planks thatched with leaves for want of straw. Others were erecting tents by adjusting over four stakes pieces of cloth found in the empty houses. Here and there, ornamenting the ground, were scattered sheep-skins, newly flayed, guitars, pitchers, wine.vessels, monks' habits, and garments of all forms and colours. In this spot troopers were sleeping quietly all armed beside their horses. Farther on, amid piles of arms foot-soldiers danced to the strains of barbarous music, grotesquely disguised with women's clothes.

When the army departed, the peasants descended from the neighbouring heights, and came from their hiding-places in every direction, as if they had risen from the bowels of the earth. They hastened homeward to their houses. Our soldiers could not stray an inch from the road, or halt a single step behind the columns, without running the risk of being instantly despatched by the revengeful mountain folk. We dared not here, as we did every where in Germany, form detached patrols, or send our sick without escort to the hospitals. Those of the infantry who were unable to march, followed their divisions mounted on asses. In their left hands they held their firelocks, and in the right their bayonets in place of crops. Like the fiery steeds of ancient Numidia, these docile animals had neither saddles nor bridles.

Chapter 3

MADRID TAKEN

On the 1st of December, we took up our night's quarters in a village about a league north of Guadalaxara. Billets were assigned us, and we were about to disband, to scatter ourselves throughout our cantonment, when we were informed that some enemy infantry were observed running at a distance. They appeared difficult to successfully attack; and a few of the youngest of the troop, obtaining leave of the colonel, began, for the love of sport, to pursue them. I marked particularly as my prize, one who ran more quickly than his fellows. He wore an azure-coloured uniform, whose brilliant colour made me take him for an officer.

When he saw that he could not escape, he stopped, and waited for me behind a ditch he had cleared with some dexterity. I believed he was then taking aim to fire at me; but on my coming within twenty yards, he dropped his weapons, doffed his hat, and with most humble reverences, in suitable attitudes, said to me, over and over —"I have the honour to salute you, *Monsuier*, I am your very humble servant." I stood, not less amazed at his comical appearance, than at hearing him speak French. I relieved him from his fears, by saying he should sustain no injury. He said he was a native of Toulouse, and a professor of dancing; and that he had been made to stand a fortnight in the pillory, so as to compel him to wear the uniform and serve in the Spanish regiment of Ferdinand VII., when the general levy took place in Andalusia; this was, as he said, altogether at odds with his gentle disposition. I told him to go to the village where our regiment was quartered, an order he did not think proper to obey. Another Frenchman was made prisoner, who was son to a principal magistrate in the town of Pau in Bearn. He was suffered to escape a few days afterwards, lest his Spanish uniform, and the arms he carried, might be recompensed at the depôt with a musket-ball.

Borne along by the pleasure of my ramble, and the ardour of my horse, I ascended first one hill, then another, crossed a torrent, and, after a smart ride of half an hour, arrived at a large village, which I entered. The inhabitants, perceiving me at a distance, were terrified lest I should be followed by others. The alarm soon spread, and they commenced in an instant to secure all their houses, by barricading, as usual, the door towards the street, and escaping over the walls of the court behind. Seeing that I was alone, they ventured out one by one, and came to the marketplace, where I had halted. I heard several men repeat, with emphasis, the word *matar*, which I conceived, as I did not understand Spanish, might be some word for expressing their wonder at the sight of a stranger. I learned afterwards that the expression means "Kill him."

These Spaniards were not quite so peaceful as the inhabitants of the German plains, where a single French soldier could govern a city. When I saw the crowd increasing, and the agitation becoming greater, I began to fear they would seize me, and deliver me to the enemy. I put spurs to my horse, and retired to a small rise behind the village, whither the men and women quickly followed. I then trotted my horse from side to side and made him leap several times over a low wall and ditch behind me, to show that I was not afraid, and could easily escape if I wished. It being the first time since we passed the Ebro that I had seen a village completely inhabited, and, above all, by females, I stayed from curiosity; and returning to my eminence, I made signs with the scabbard of my sabre, that none of them, for they again approached me, should come nearer than ten paces. I then endeavoured to make them understand that my horse wanted something to eat. The inhabitants, muffled in their cloaks, looked at me in silent astonishment. They maintained, however, all the while, that characteristic gravity, and dignity of look and manner, which distinguish Castilians of every age and rank. They appeared to regard a stranger with profound contempt, for his ignorance of their language.

When I saw there was no chance of being understood, I attempted some words of Latin. We often found that language useful in Spain, in making ourselves understood by the clergy, who, in general, speak it tolerably well. A young student then left the crowd, and returned a few moments afterwards with the village schoolmaster. This personage was so happy to speak Latin, and to inform me how he had arrived at such a high degree of knowledge, that he enabled me to procure every thing I wanted, and I departed soon after. So early as next morning, when our regiment passed through the same village, it was completely deserted. I lost my way in the dark in returning to our cantonment, and it was midnight before I rejoined my companions.

Next day, December 2nd, we removed our quarters to the neighbourhood of Alcala de Henares. On our way we fell in with a squadron of Polish lancers, which Marshal Bessieres had despatched from St Augustin to reconnoitre in the direction of Guadalaxara. They informed us that the advanced guard of the central army had reached Madrid. Our distance from it was not less than three leagues.

The Emperor Napoleon had left Burgos for Aranda on the 22nd November, to direct the movements of his army of the left on the Ebro, against the right of the Spaniards, and to sustain them, if assistance should be required. On the 29th November, seven days after the action at Tudela, he had marched the army of the centre against Madrid in the direction of the Castiles. The corps of Marshal Soult remained in the Asturias, to watch the remains of the Spanish army of Gallicia. On the 30th, at day-break, the advanced guard of the Emperor's army arrived at the foot of the mountain Somo Sierra. The *puerto*, or pass of this mountain, was defended by a force of from twelve to fifteen thousand Spaniards, and a battery of sixteen pieces of cannon. Three regiments of infantry of our first division, and six pieces of cannon, commenced the attack. The Polish lancers of the guard then charged the pass, and carried the enemy's battery by storm. The Spaniards, unable to resist Napoleon, fled on every side, and took refuge among the rocks. The Imperial headquarters were taken up, on the 1st of December, at St Augustin. The corps of Marshal Ney, to which our regiment belonged, came by Guadalaxara and Alcala the same day to join the army of the Emperor.

On the morning of December 2nd, Napoleon accompanied by his cavalry alone, went in advance of the army, and positioned himself on the heights that overlook the Spanish capital. Instead of the regularity usually exhibited in fortified cities, where every event of war is provided for—in place of that silence which is only broken by the deep prolonged sounds of "Sentry, have a care!" by which the sentinels on the ramparts keep awake each other's vigilance; there were heard only the continual pealing of the bells of the six hundred churches of Madrid, and at intervals the loud uproar of the rabble, and the furious beating of drums.

The inhabitants of Madrid never thought of defence till eight days before the arrival of the French, and all their preparations displayed inexperience and haste. They had placed their artillery behind temporary ramparts and *barricadoes*, or had erected hasty fortifications by piling together bales of wool and cotton. The windows of the houses, at the entrance of the principal streets, were occupied by soldiers screened behind mattresses. The only place fortified with any care was the *Retiro*, a royal castle, seated on the hill which commands the capital. According to custom, an aid-de-camp of Marshal Bessieres was sent in the morning to summon Madrid. He was within a hair's breadth of being torn to pieces by the inhabitants, because he had proposed their surrender to the French, and only escaped by the protection he received from the regular Spanish troops.

The evening of that day was spent by the Emperor in reconnoitring around the city, and arranging his plan of attack. At seven o clock in the evening, the advanced columns of infantry having arrived, a brigade of the First Corps, supported by four pieces of artillery, marched against the suburbs. The *tirailleurs* of the 16th regiment, having dislodged the Spaniards from some advanced houses, made themselves masters of the principal burial-ground. The night was occupied in positioning the artillery, and making the necessary preparations for an attack next day.

A Spanish officer, taken at Somo Sierra was sent by the Prince of Neufchatel, at midnight, into Madrid. He returned, some hours after, with the information that the inhabitants were still determined to resist. The cannonade, therefore, commenced on the morning of the 3rd, at 9 o'clock.

Thirty pieces of cannon, under the command of General Cenarmont, battered down a breach in the wall of the *Retiro*, whilst twenty pieces of Imperial Guard artillery, and some light troops, made a feigned attack in another direction, to divert the attention and divide the strength of the enemy. The light company of Vilatte's division entered by the breach into the garden of the *Retiro*, and were soon followed by their battalion. In less than an hour, the 4000 Spanish troops of the line, who defended that principal post, were overpowered. By eleven o clock, our soldiers were already in possession of the important posts of the observatory, the porcelain factory, the main barracks, and the palace of Medina Coeli. Masters of all the *Retiro*, we could have burned Madrid in a few hours.

The cannonade then ceased to be heard. In every quarter the further progress of the troops was arrested, and for a third time a messenger was despatched to conduct a parley with the place. It was of no small importance to the Emperor to spare the capital of the kingdom he designed for his brother. It is possible to establish a camp, but not a court, amidst ruins. Madrid, reduced to ashes, might have stimulated, by its example, every other city of the kingdom to a desperate resistance. The French armies would also have been deprived of vast resources by its destruction.

In the afternoon, about five o'clock, the French envoy returned, accompanied by General Morla, the chief of the military junta, and Don B. Yriarte, representing the town. They were conducted to the tent of the Prince de Neufchatel. They requested that a suspension of hostilities during be granted to them, to allow them an opportunity to persuade the people to surrender. The Emperor assumed the appearance of great anger, reproached them for having failed in fulfilling the terms of the treaty of Baylen, and for the massacre of the French prisoners in Andalusia. It was his wish, by acting thus, to terrify the Spanish deputies, so that on returning, they would impart their fear of the Emperor's anger and the consequences of incurring it to those who obeyed their orders. He was most anxious that the surrender of Madrid should appear to be voluntary. It was believed that the example of the capital would then be followed by the whole of Spain.

In the meantime, the townsmen refused to lay down their arms, and still continued to fire on the French from the windows of the houses which surround the Prado promenade. We were informed by the prisoners, that were continually pouring in, that fear and frenzy were reigning throughout the city. Fifty thousand armed citizens were ranging about the streets without discipline, demanding leadership, and accusing their governors of treason. The Captain-General, Marquis de Castellar, and all the military men of any note, abandoned Madrid with the troops of the line, and six pieces of artillery during the night. At six o clock in the morning of the 4th of December, General Morla and Don F. de Vera came again to the tent of Prince Neufchatel, and at ten o'clock a.m., the French soldiers took possession of Madrid.

The Emperor remained with his guard encamped on the hill of Chamartin. The very day Madrid was taken, he sent numerous detachments in all directions, according to his usual plan of military operations, that the enemy might have no time to recover; and to take advantage of the surprise and panic, which seldom fail, after great events, to double the conqueror's strength, while they paralyze that of the conquered. Marshal Bessieres, with six squadrons, pursued, on the road to Valencia, the Spanish army of General la Penna. This force was compelled by General Ruffin's division of infantry, and General Bordesoult's brigade of dragoon, to turn back towards Cuença. The corps of Marshal Victor went by way of Aranjuez to Toledo. The cavalry of Generals Lasalle and Milhaud went in pursuit of the scattered troops repulsed at Somo Sierra, and those that had escaped from Madrid. General Houssaye entered the Escurial.

Our regiment of Hussars had been stationed around Alcala since the 2nd of December, about three leagues from Madrid. On the 5th, we were ordered to appear early at the Imperial quarters, for the purpose of being reviewed. We had not arrived many minutes, in a plain near the Chateau de Chamartin, when Napoleon suddenly made his appearance. He was attended by the Prince de Neufchatel, and five or six aides-de-camp, who could scarcely keep up with him, he rode so fast. All the trumpets sounded. The Emperor halted about a hundred paces from the front of the centre of our regiment, and demanded from the Colonel the list of the officers, subalterns, and privates, who had merited military honours. The Colonel of the regiment having quickly called them by name, Napoleon addressed a few words familiarly to some of the common soldiers who were presented to him; but, turning again to the General who commanded our brigade, he put two or three short questions to him in a hurried manner. The General not replying very concisely, Napoleon turned his horse without hearing him finish his speech, and took his departure as unexpectedly and swiftly as he had arrived.

The review being over, we prepared to enter Madrid. A heavy silence had succeeded that confusion and uproar which had reigned within and without the walls of the capital only the day before. The streets through which we entered were deserted; and even in the market-place, the numerous shops of the vendors of necessaries still remained shut. The water-carriers were the only people of the town who had not interrupted their usual avocations. They moved about uttering their cries with the nasal drawling tone, peculiar to their native mountains of Galicia, "*Quien quiere agua?*"—"Who wants water?" No purchasers made their appearance; the waterman muttered to himself sorrowfully, "*Dios que la da*"—"It is God's gift," and cried again.

As we advanced into the heart of the city, we perceived groups of Spaniards standing at the corner of a square, where they had formerly been in the habit of assembling in great numbers. They stood muffled in their capacious cloaks, regarding us with a sullen dejected aspect. Their national pride could scarcely let them credit, that any other then Spanish soldiers could have beaten Spaniards. If they happened to perceive among our ranks a horse which had once belonged to their cavalry, they soon distinguished him by his pace, and awakening from their apathy, would whisper together, "*Este cavallo es Espagnole*"—"That's a Spanish horse;" as if they had discovered the sole cause of our success.

We passed quite through Madrid. Our regiment proceeded to canton for sixteen days at Cevolla, near the Tagus, in the direction of Talavera. We returned again on the 19th of December, to form part of the garrison of Madrid. The inhabitants in and around the capital had by that time recovered from their astonishment. The sight of the French had, by degrees, become familiar to them. The strictest discipline was observed by the army; and tranquillity, at least in appearance, prevailed as much as in time of peace.

On entering Madrid in the morning by the gate of Toledo, or the Place de la Cenada, where the market is held, nothing is more striking than the confused mass of people from the country and provinces, who, variously clad, are arriving and departing, going and coming. There, a Castilian draws around him with dignity the folds of his ample cloak, like a Roman senator in his toga. Here a cowherd from La Mancha, with his long goad in his hand, clad in a kilt of ox-skin, whose antique shape bears some resemblance to the tunic worn by the Roman and Gothic warriors. Farther on, may be seen men with their hair confined in long nets of silk. Others, wearing a kind of short brown vest, striped with blue and red, conveying the idea of the Moorish garb. The men who wear this dress come from Andalusia. They are remarkable for their lively black eyes, their rapid utterance, and expressive animated countenances. At the corners of the streets and places of resort, are to be seen women preparing refreshments for all those who have no permanent abode in Madrid.

On arriving, we observed long trains of mules, laden with skins, containing wine and oil; and large droves of asses under the care of one per son, who spoke to them incessantly. We met also carriages drawn by eight or ten mules, ornamented with small bells. A single coachman guided them either at trot or gallop with great dexterity, making no use of reins, and urging them forward with his voice alone, shouting most savagely. These mules are trained all to stop at the same instant by one long shrill whistle. They might be mistaken for teams of stags or elks, by their long taper legs, the height of their stature, and the bold lofty carriage of their heads. The shouts of the coach-drivers and muleteers — the constant chiming of the bells of the churches — the various dresses of the men — the extravagant display of southern energy evinced in their gestures and loud sonorous cries in a language we did not understand — their manners so unlike one own; — all contributed to give to the Spanish capital a most strange appearance to people accustomed to the quietness with which all is done in the north. We were the more struck with it, because Madrid was the first large city we found inhabited since we entered Spain.

At the hour of *siesta*, and more particularly in summer,

during the heat of the day, all this uproar ceased, and the whole city resigned itself to sleep. The only sound then heard in the streets was from the trampling of the horses of some of our own troops of cavalry returning from or going their rounds, or the drum of some detachment of infantry about to mount the solitary guard. That drum had already beaten the march and the charge in Alexandria, in Cairo, in Rome, and almost in every city of Europe from Konigsberg to Madrid.

Our regiment continued nearly a whole month in the Spanish capital. I stayed with an old man from a distinguished family, who lived alone with his daughter. He went regularly twice a day to mass, and once to the Place del Sol, to hear the news. On returning, he seated himself in his parlour, where he spent the whole day doing nothing. Sometimes he would light a cigar, and puff away, in smoke, his weariness and his woes. He seldom spoke, and I never saw him laugh. He only exclaimed, at intervals of half an hour, with a heavy sigh, "Ah Jesus!" His daughter constantly replied in the same words, and both were again silent.

Every day my entertainers were visited by a priest, the holy father of the household, who was as assiduous in his attentions as physicians in some countries are to their patients. He wore a flax-coloured wig to conceal his priestly tonsure, and was dressed like an ordinary citizen, always insinuating, that he dared not wear his sacerdotal habit for fear of being assassinated in the streets by the French. This unnecessary deception was solely designed to increase the bitter animosity which already existed against us.

Notwithstanding the appearance of most profound tranquillity reigning in the capital, our regiment were always prepared to mount instantly; and, as if we had been an advanced post, with the enemy before us, our horses never were unsaddled. It was indeed reported, that eleven hundred Spanish desperadoes remained concealed in the city when it capitulated, waiting only a favourable opportunity to raise the inhabitants in arms, and put every Frenchman to the sword.

Amid the plaudits of victory resounded by our bulletins, we could not help entertaining a feeling of perplexed uncertainty about the very advantages we had obtained. It was observed by someone, that our conquests lay above volcanoes. The Emperor Napoleon did not make a public entry into Madrid, as he had done into other European capitals. The forms of etiquette under which he subjected himself towards his brother Joseph, whom he already considered an independent sovereign, prevented him from observing this ceremony. Constantly encamped with his Guard on the heights of Chamartin, he daily prescribed decrees to Spain, waiting that submission which it was natural to think would soon be effected by the terror of our rapid successes.

The thundering proclamations issued by the Emperor, announced his triumphs to an astonished Europe, and gave to such places of the Peninsula as persevered in their resistance much cause to dread a terrible destiny. And yet the several provinces of Spain displayed no promptness in taking steps to propitiate the implacable conqueror, or avert the death-blow they had reason to dread. No-one offered to lay at Napoleon's feet, with the exacted homage, that fawning praise to which other countries had accustomed him. Deputations from the city of Madrid, and the Alcaids of some places occupied by our troops, alone came to present submissions extorted by fear, at the Imperial quarters of Chamartin. The heads of twelve hundred select families in Madrid being summoned, also appeared to take the oath of fidelity to King Joseph. But it was even said, that the very priests, before whom they swore on the Gospels, had given them advance absolution for every forced oath of subjection they might make to their conquerors.

The declarations made by the French authorities, that they came to reduce the religious orders, and abolish the Inquisition, far from placing us in the light of saviours, tended only to worsen that bitter hatred which the clergy and their numerous zealots already bore us. The friars of every order who had been exiled from their convents, spread over the country, and, wherever they went, preached against us. Disguising, by a holy zeal, their resentment for the recent loss of their wealth, they endeavoured, by every means in their power, to stimulate the people against the French. The priests protested warmly, that it was against strangers alone that the Inquisition was upheld and that, without it, the principles of religion would long since have been as completely ruined in Spain, as for more than twenty years they had now been in France.

For a century past, the Inquisition had indeed been made more tolerable. It no longer was the terror of Spaniards; and some intelligent individuals had even gone so far as to consider it essential to a feeble government, for restraining the multitude, and curbing the power of the inferior clergy. The poor began to reflect where they would have to go, in seasons of scarcity, for that sustenance they had been accustomed to receive every day at the convent gates.

A superstitious nation like this, which supposed its establishments had always existed, could not conceive how they should ever terminate. In the times of their misfortune, therefore, every change effected by an enemy appeared downright impiety.

Chapter 4

THE ENGLISH ARRIVE

Some days after Madrid surrendered, while our regiment
was quartered at Cevolla on the Tagus, I received orders to
carry an open despatch to Marshal Lefevre from General
Lasalle, who lay in our front at Talavera. Marshal Lefevre
was to read the despatch, and then forward it to the Prince
of Neufchatel. At Maqueda I met Marshal Lefevre, as the
sun went down, just arriving from Casa Rubios. To spare
his own aides-de-camp, he commanded me to prosecute
the journey myself, and deliver, at the Imperial quarters, the
letters I had in charge. Requiring to ride post, I mounted a
requisition-mule, which the staff-major made the *Alcaid* of
the place provide for me.

I was soon on my way, in a dismal night, on a huge ob-
stinate mule, whose mane somebody had shorn, preceded
by a Spanish peasant, riding a mule that matched my own.
When we had gone about a league, my guide allowed
himself to fall, and his beast started off at the gallop, to
return, I suppose, to the village. Thinking the poor fellow
had fainted by the violence of his fall, I alighted to render
him assistance. In vain I sought for him, where I imagined
he had fallen; the rogue had slipped into the thick brushwood, and disappeared. I mounted my mule again, uncertain of my road; The wicked animal, no longer hearing its
companion, would now go neither one way nor another.

The more I spurred him, the more he kicked, My blows, abuses, and French menaces, only enraged him. I did not know his name, and was not then even aware that every Spanish mule has a name; or that to make any progress, I should have said, "Get on, mule; go on, Captain; get along, Arragonese," &c. Dismounting, to tighten the girth of my wooden saddle, the passionate animal reared, struck me on the breast a blow which knocked me to the ground, and then turned into a side-path. As soon as I recovered, I pursued him with all my might, directed by the noise my stirrups made on the stones, my saddle having turned round. After running half a league I found my saddle, from which the mule had disencumbered himself. I took it on my back, and soon after entered a large village, where the van-guard of one of Lefevre's brigades had arrived. I made the *Alcaid* give me a horse, and again took the road, with especial care to keep close to my guide.

There was no French garrison in the place where I next changed horses. The master of the post-house, a lively, fresh old man, opened the door to me himself. He awoke a postilion, and directed him to saddle an old horse, whose crooked forelegs could scarcely bear his weight. I uttered some threats against the postmaster, and, raising my voice, signified which horse I wished to ride. The old fellow was not to be frightened; but, with a mildness which allayed my passion in a moment, took me by the hand, and, making a sign to be silent, he showed me thirty or forty peasants asleep among a heap of chopped straw, at the other end of the stable. I took the benefit of his advice and mounted the horse, bad as it was, without a word; admiring the generous feeling this little action displayed, and musing on the countless difficulties of the situation, to which we were subjected by Spanish hatred, even now when we were every where victorious.

I reached the Imperial quarters at Chamartin by one o'clock next morning. One of his aides-de-camp awoke the Prince of Neufchatel. I delivered my letters to him, and, at eleven the same night, was sent back to my own corps, with new despatches for Marshal Victor. It was morning when I arrived at Aranjuez. The commandant of the place advised me to delay my journey to Toledo, for the march of a detachment going thither. The director of the posts of the first corps, having preceded his convoy but a few minutes, had been butchered on the road the evening before. But as I was instructed to expedite my orders without delay, I continued my journey, mounted on a requisitioned pony. Being alone, I was compelled to discharge myself the duties of rearguard, vanguard, and flank, galloping up the heights, and keeping a constant look out, that I might not be taken by surprise. The wild horses of the royal stud, with the deer and stags, in herds of from fifty to sixty, fled as I approached.

Some leagues beyond Aranjuez, I observed two peasants at a distance, who had bound a soldier, and were dragging him into the brushwood, to put him to death. With the full speed of my horse, I rode towards them, and happily arrived in time to rescue the unfortunate prisoner. He proved to be an infantryman, who had left Aranjuez hospital the day before. Overpowered with fatigue, he had sat down to recover himself, whilst his comrades continued their march. I escorted him to his detachment, which had halted not far distant, and proceeded on my way.

Nothing can exceed the horrible sight I next beheld. At every step I stumbled over the disfigured bodies of Frenchmen, recently murdered, and bloody shreds of their garments. The still vivid marks in the sand, declared how some of these hapless beings must have wrestled, and the prolonged torments they must have endured, before they expired. The copper-plates of their caps, scattered around, could alone show that they had been soldiers, or to what regiments they belonged. Those who had thus attacked the French on the Toledo road, were the keepers of the Royal stud, and some peasants who had abandoned their villages on the arrival of our troops. They had acquired a high degree of barbarity by their vagabond and solitary way of living.

I had delivered my despatches to Marshal Victor at Toledo, and was returned to my regiment, the day before it went to garrison Madrid.

The Spaniards of the plains of Castile were already recovering from the temporary dread occasioned by our arrival. The inhabitants of the places we occupied, had retired to the mountains and woods with their wives and infants. They espied from thence all our movements, and lay in ambush near our principal routes, to intercept our couriers and our orders; or to assault unexpectedly such of our detachments as they believed were weaker than themselves.

Not a day passed, without bringing us disastrous intelligence of some of the small parties left behind to preserve our communications. All our communication posts, stationed in our rear as in Germany, and consisting of only nine or fifteen men, were annihilated.

The Spanish Junta had retired to Merida, and from thence had gone to Seville. It then sent orders to the *Alcaids* and clergy, even of the places we occupied, to invite the soldiers of the Spanish militia to join their respective corps. These soldiers of their country, seeking to avoid our troops, travelled by night through unfrequented paths; and thus the dispersed Spanish armies constantly recovered from their disasters, with wonderful celerity and ease. When the army of Castanos arrived at Cuença after its defeat at Tudela, it was reduced to 9000 infantry and 2000 cavalry. One mouth afterwards, at the engagement of Ucles, the same army numbered more than 25,000 men. After the defeat of General Blake at Espinosa, the Marquis of Romana could scarcely bring together 5000 soldiers in Galicia. By the beginning of December, he had 22,000 recruits around the city of Leon. Although the Spanish Junta was but a weak and powerless administration, it notwithstanding possessed considerable influence, when it acted in the path of the nation's choice. The operations, which were wholly spontaneous, were proportionally permanent. The Spanish generals, like their government, had authority only when they acted with the approval of those they commanded. They could neither restrain their soldiers when conquerors, nor rally them when defeated; and these undisciplined bands bore their generals along with them, in the rush of their victory or flight. Their Spanish pride was so great, that they would never attribute their losses to their own inexperience, or the superior discipline of their enemies. Whenever they were beaten, they accused their commanders of treason. General St Juan was hanged by his soldiers at Talavera; General la Penna was supplanted by the divisions of Andalusia; and the Duke de l'Infantado was obliged to take the command of the army at Cuença.

The Spaniards were a religious and brave people, but devoid of military genius. They even hated and condemned every thing relating to troops of the line. They were thus in want of superior and subaltern officers, and all that constitutes a well regulated army. They regarded their present contest as a religious crusade against the French, for their country and their king. A red riband, with this inscription, *Vincer O Morir Pro Patria Et Pro Ferdinando Septimo*,— "Conquer or die for our native land and Ferdinand VII" was the only military distinction of the greater part of these citizen-soldiers. At the first summons, men, almost naked, repaired from every province to the great assemblies that they styled their armies. There, the ardent desire of conquest with which they were inspired, made them endure with admirable patience such privations as all the power of the severest discipline could never have compelled regular troops to undergo.

In general, the people of the provinces manifested much scepticism about the successes we obtained even when we were victorious. No Spaniard would give credit to the misfortunes of Spain, or believe she could be subdued. This sentiment, which animated every heart, rendered the nation invincible, in defiance of individual losses, and the frequent discomfiture of her armies.

The English entered Spain about the end of the year 1808. On the 14th of October, 13,000 soldiers, commanded by General Sir David Baird, had disembarked at Corunna, and advanced by Lugo to Astorga Another army, under General Moore, Commander-in-chief of all the British forces, had marched from Lisbon on the 27th of the same month. It had arrived at Estremadura and the Castiles, by the routes of Almeida, Ciudad Rodrigo, Alcantara, and Merida. The division that marched by Merida had advanced on the 22nd of November as far as the Escurial. All the English corps in the Peninsula were to unite at Salamanca and Valadolid, and reinforce the Spanish army before Burgos. When that army was dispersed, as well as General Blake's in the Asturias, General Sir David Baird fell back from Astorga to Villa Franca. Afterwards, when the French marched upon Madrid, subsequently to the engagement at Tudela, General Moore recalled the division of the English which had advanced to the Escurial, and concentrated his army in the environs of Salamanca. The English armies in Spain remained nearly a month at Villa

Franca and Salamanca, irresolute what course they should follow. They dared neither advance against the vast power of the French in front, nor retreat, from the fear of discouraging the people of Spain, and extinguishing the national spirit, which still survived in spite of the severest trials.

Some misunderstanding existed at this time between the English and Spaniards, and caused a want of concord in their military operations. The Spaniards, not considering that the English were only auxiliaries in their quarrel, reproached them at first for the tardiness of their marches, and afterwards for their inactivity. The English General, in his turn, accused the Spaniards of having uniformly dissembled their real condition and misfortunes, and having always exaggerated their powers of resistance. Like the French Commander, he misapprehended the Spanish character, and generally regarded as imbecility all that patriotism made a nation, devoid of military resources, believe, declare, and perform; strong, however, in their patriotic spirit, and indomitable from the very causes which made them gloss over their disasters.

The Spaniards even went so far as to believe that the English wished to abandon them to their fate. The French also, in accordance with the general opinion, believed that the English had no other intention but to re-embark at Lisbon or Corunna. Marshal Lefevre was even sent forward from Talavera, to menace the communications of General Moore, and oblige him hastily to descend the Tagus. General Soult, who had remained on the frontiers of the kingdom of Leon, also prepared to enter Galicia, and was to be reinforced by the corps of General Junot, which had arrived from France, and was advancing toward Burgos.

Whilst matters proceeded thus, intelligence was brought to the Imperial quarters at Chamartin, that at Rueda, one of the posts of General Franchesci had been carried on the 12th, and that detachments of English were scouring the country, even to the gates of Valladolid.

These were advanced parties of General Moore's army, which had left Salamanca on the 13th of December, and had passed the Douro to effect a junction with 13,000 English, whom General Sir David Baird was bringing from Villa Franca. They had planned a combined attack, in conjunction with the Spanish troops of the Marquis de la Romana, against Marshal Soult, who, with 15,000 men, occupied the small towns of Guarda, Saldanna, and Sahagun, on the banks of the river Coa. A brigade of cavalry, under General Paget, on the 21st, attacked and defeated a regiment of French Dragoons that Marshal Soult had left at Sahagun.

The Emperor Napoleon being informed of these movements of the English, commenced his march from Madrid on the 22nd with his guards, and the corps of Marshal Ney, to cut off their retreat to Corunna. He arrived at Villa Castin on the 23rd, at Tordesillas on the 25th, at Medina de Rio Seco on the 27th; and, on the morning of December 29th, his advanced guard, consisting of three squadrons of Chasseurs à Cheval, commanded by General Lefevre, came up with the English in Benevente.

General Lefevre, finding the bridge over the Esla destroyed, passed the river by the ford, and drove in the English out-posts to the very gates of the city. The General, borne along by the ardour of pursuit, omitted to draw off his Chasseurs, or make his observations, and was suddenly attacked by the whole cavalry of the enemy. Our cavalry were compelled to repass the Esla, sixty men being wounded or dismounted, and their General a prisoner. Having gained the bank, they formed for the charge, and prepared to make a desperate effort to rescue their captive leader. But the English hastily brought up two pieces of light artillery near the broken bridge, and, opening a fire of grape-shot, made the French squadrons retire.

The Anglo-Spanish army had received advice of the Emperor Napoleon's march, just as they were meditating an attack on Marshal Soult, at the village of Carrion. On the 24th, they were retiring rapidly towards Astorga and Benevente, by Mayorga, Valencia, and Mancilla. They would most likely have been cut off from the passes of Galicia, if the French army had not been considerably obstructed in its march by the swollen torrents, and the snow lately fallen about the Sierra de Guadarama.

The Emperor Napoleon arrived on the 30th of December at Benevente, and having proceeded no farther than Astorga, returned on the 7th of January to Valladolid with his guards. A few days afterwards, he was in France, making preparations to march against Austria. Marshal Ney was left at Astorga, to secure the passes of Galicia, and organize the country. Marshal Soult continued the pursuit of General Moore's army towards Corunna. The English, in their retreat, left the country behind them a total desert, and the troops of Marshal Soult were every evening obliged to forage at great distances from the line of march, which greatly retarded their progress, and increased their fatigue. His advance guard, notwithstanding, came up with the enemy's rear at Villa Franca, and again at Lugo, but did not think themselves sufficiently strong to commence an attack. The French lost General Colbert of the cavalry, in a skirmish which happened before the former of these towns.

On the 16th, the English were obliged to engage before Corunna, previous to their embarkation. The battle was bloody, and keenly contested. At first the French gained ground, but towards evening the English recovered the commanding position which they had originally occupied, to cover the anchorage of their fleet. During the night, between the 16th and 17th, they embarked. General Moore was struck by a cannon-ball as he led back again to the charge a corps which had been repulsed. The army of the Marquis de la Romana had broken up among the mountains to the west of Astorga. Corunna, being a fortified town, was defended by its inhabitants, and did not surrender till the 29th by capitulation.

The English, in their retreat, endured all the hardships to which armies hotly pursued are exposed, when the toils of the soldiers have enraged them out of measure. Without having fought one pitched battle, they lost more than 8000 men, and almost all the horses of their cavalry.

One cannot well conceive what motives influenced General Moore to hazard the fate of his whole army by an expedition against the corps of Marshal Soult, the result of which every way could only be most doubtful. The Marshal could easily have fallen back on Burgos, and been reinforced by the troops of General Junot. General Moore, in marching to Saldanna, gave Napoleon an opportunity of attacking him with all his forces united, when the Emperor was preparing to return to France. He might have moved from Salamanca, to a position almost impregnable behind the bridge of Almarez on the Tagus, and reorganized the armies of Spain. This was what the French chiefly dreaded. In leaving Salamanca, General Moore ought at any rate to have retreated rather to Lisbon than Corunna, taking the shortest route, and leaving to Marshals Lefevre and Soult the most extended line of communications, to guard which they must have weakened themselves considerably, by posting detachments in their rear. He could thus also have enabled the troops of General de la Romana, and the peasants of Galicia and

Portugal, frequently to harass the French in a desultory warfare. This latter operation has since been accomplished with the most complete Success, by General Sir Arthur Wellesley—now Duke of Wellington.

It is affirmed that General Moore was deceived by false information, and that it was against his own opinion and contrary to his will, he was made to deviate on this occasion from the established rules of military science. Besides, it is an easy matter to judge of actions after they have happened; the difficulty of any undertaking consists in foreseeing its probable issue.

Whilst the corps of Marshal Soult was thus expelling the English from Galicia, the Spanish army of Andalusia was making various movements in advance of Cuença, by which Madrid seemed to be menaced. To oppose this Spanish force, commanded by the Duke de l'Infantado, Marshal Victor on the 10th of January left Toledo with the first corps of the army. For several days they advanced slowly in the neighbourhood of Ocana, without any intelligence of the enemy. Whether by chance, or from ignorance of the country, the French divisions found themselves on the morning of the 13th so entangled among the Spaniards, that so far from expecting to turn them, they themselves conceived they were surrounded.

The division of Villate first engaged with part of the enemy's force, drawn up in order of battle, on the top of a steep and lofty eminence. The Spaniards had more faith in the strength of their position than in the skill of their troops, most of whom were newly raised. But when they beheld the ardour and coolness with which the French under arms ascended the rocks, they fled after firing a single discharge. Near Alcazar they met in their retreat the division of Ruffin, which unexpectedly turned the enemy while it was only seeking for them. Some thousand Spaniards were forced to surrender; surprise and terror took possession of their whole army, and the different corps of which it was composed were thrown into complete disorder. Several of their columns endeavouring to escape, ran headlong on General Cenarmont's park of artillery, and were received by a discharge of grape-shot which compelled them to face-about. A piece of French artillery, the horses of which were exhausted, was met by the enemy's cavalry. They made way for it, and filed off in respectful silence on each side of the road. The French took more than 10,000 prisoners, and 40 pieces of cannon, which the Spaniards abandoned in their flight, if the Dragoons of General Latour Maubourg had not been too fatigued for pursuit, the whole Spanish army must have fallen into our power.

On the 13th of January, the day on which the fight at Ucles happened, our regiment left Madrid for the purpose of rejoining the first corps d'armée. On the 14th we lay at Ocana. On the morning of the 15th, about three leagues from this town, we fell in with the Spanish prisoners taken at Ucles, who were going to Madrid. Some of these poor wretches expired from hunger; many of them sunk down exhausted with fatigue: and when they were unable to go farther, they were mercilessly shot. This sanguinary order was given in retaliation for the death of the French prisoners whom the Spaniards hanged. This inhuman conduct, unseasonably exercised against disarmed foes, whose helplessness entitled them to clemency, could on no account be justified by the necessity of reprisal. Besides, if the grand design of conquest be the lasting submission of the conquered, the measures, as impolitic as cruel, tend greatly to distance this desirable end. No doubt, the Spanish peasants were thus deterred from joining their armies. But the consequence of this was, that an ambuscade warfare succeeded regular battles, where our decided superiority of tactics would likely always have enabled us to triumph. Our clemency would thus have perfected the submission of those whom our arms had already half subdued. As it was, the French, with only 400,090 men, had to contend with twelve millions of people inflamed with hatred, despair, and revenge.

Our attention was particularly attracted by one of these unhappy Spaniards. He was lying on his back, mortally wounded. We saw, from his long black mustachios, intermingled with gray hairs, and his uniform, that he was a veteran soldier. The only sounds we could hear him utter, were a few words of invocation to the Virgin and the Saints. We tried to revive him with a little brandy, but a few moments after he expired.

Nothing can be more appalling than to follow the track of a victorious army. As we had not shared in the success of our comrades, who had just beaten the enemy before us, so no remembrance of our own dangers, fatigues, or anxieties, could diminish the horror of the spectacles we witnessed. We travelled through a desolated and deserted country; we lodged indiscriminately beside the dying and the dead, who had crawled from the gory field of battle to the nearest houses, to close their eyes forever, unassisted and unseen.

We joined our division at Cuença, and took up our quarters for a few days in the neighbourhood of Belmonte and San Clemente. We had to wait for our artillery, which could not, without much difficulty, make out more than one or two leagues a day. The rains of winter had made the roads so bad, that it was often necessary to take the teams of several pieces of artillery to drag a single gun. We afterwards crossed Don Quixote's country in going to Consuegra and Madrilejos. Toboso exactly corresponds with the description given of it by Cervantes, in his immortal romance of *Don Quixote de La Mancha*. If that visionary hero did not render great service to widows and orphans while he lived, his memory at least preserved from the horrors of war the country of his imaginary Dulcinea. The first woman the French soldiers saw at a window, they cried out, laughing, "There's Dulcinea!" Their mirth emboldened the inhabitants; and, far from flying, as usual, at the sight of our advanced guard, they collected to see us pass. Jests about Dulcinea and Don Quixote formed a link of connexion between us and the citizens of Toboso; and the French, being well entertained, treated in their turn their hosts with urbanity.

We remained for more than a month quartered in La Mancha. Our mode of living was whether we staid in houses or bivouacked in the field; only, in place of removing from one house to another, we went from our own fire to that of our comrades. There we spent the tedious night, quenching our thirst, and conversing about the occurrences of the war, or listening to the account of past campaigns. Sometimes about daybreak, a horse pinched with the chillness of the dews, would pull up his stake, and come gently to the fire and warm his nose, as if the old servant was reminding us that he too had a share in the engagement about which we were speaking.

The simple stirring life we led had both its pleasures and its dangers. Every hour, when near the enemy, we were seeing detachments going and coming after long absence, and bringing news of others in Spain at a great distance.

When we were ordered to be in readiness to ride, we might as well have been sent to France, Germany, or the extremity of Europe, as on a short excursion to the neighbourhood. When we left a place, we could not tell if we might ever return. When we halted at any spot, we knew not if our stay might be for months, or for hours. The longest, dreariest stay was never wearisome, because we always expected something new. We were often destitute of daily bread; but our comfort in our distress was the hope of an approaching change. When abundance returned to us, we hastened to enjoy it; we lived fast; we made up for past abstinence, and kept in remembrance that our plenty must pass away. When the thunder of artillery in the distance announced that a battle was near—when the different divisions hurried to the place of action, and brothers and friends that had been separated distinguished each other—they would stop to embrace and utter a transient *adieu*: their arms would clash, their plumes would intertwine, and, they would tear themselves asunder to rejoin their ranks.

The frequency of danger made us regard death as one of the most common occurrences. We grieved for our comrades when wounded, but if dead, we showed an indifference about them that often bordered on levity. When the soldiers, in passing, recognised a companion numbered with the slain, they would say, " He is now above want, he will abuse his horse no more, his drinking days are done"—or words to that purpose; which manifested a stoical disregard of existence. It was the only funeral oration spoken over the warriors that had fallen.

The different regiments of our army, particularly the cavalry and infantry, were considerably distinguished from each other in their customs and manners. The infantry, having nothing else to occupy their attention but themselves and their muskets, were great egotists, talkers and sleepers. Doomed, during war, to face death unshrinking, under terror of disgrace, they displayed a fierceness in their hostility, and a disposition to make others suffer, when they could, the evils themselves had endured. They were often impertinent, and sometimes even insolent, to their officers; but in the midst of almost insupportable hardships, a *bon-mot* would restore them to reason, and set them a laughing. They forgot all their toils the moment they heard the enemy's fire.

The Hussars, and Chasseurs à Cheval, were accustomed of being, for the most part, plunderers, wasters, and drinkers and of taking every license in the presence of an enemy. Accustomed, it may be said, to sleep with one eye open, to keep always one ear awake to the sound of the alarm-trumpet, to reconnoitre in a march far in advance of the army, to anticipate the snares of the enemy, to discover the slightest traces of their course, to scour the ravines, and to survey with eagle-eye the distant plains,—they could not but acquire a superior intelligence, and a habit of self-management. And yet they were always silent, and submissive before their officers, from the dread of being unhorsed.

Everlastingly smoking to pass away his time, the light-horseman braved in every country the severity of the climate, under his capacious cloak. The horse and his rider, habituated to each other's company, contracted an affinity of feeling. The trooper was invigorated by his horse, and the horse by his master. When a Hussar, scarcely sober, urged his fleet career among ravines, or in the midst of precipices, the horse usurped all the management which the man in his senses possessed; it would curb its ardour, redouble its caution, shun every danger, and always return, after a few evolutions, to fill up its own and its master's place in the ranks. Sometimes on a journey, the horse would gently slacken its pace, or even incline itself to either side, so as to retain its inebriated and sleeping master in the saddle. The Hussar, awaking from this unseasonable lethargy, seeing his horse breathless with exertion, would lament, vow, and swear never to drink more. For several days he would act the pedestrian, and deprive himself of his own provisions to share them with his fellow-traveller.

When the alarm was given in a camp of light cavalry, by a carbine shot from the videttes, in the twinkling of an eye every horse was bridled, and horsemen might be seen in all directions springing through the bivouac fires, leaping over hedges and ditches, and hastening with the speed of lightning to the rendezvous, to repel the first attack of the enemy. The trumpeter's horse alone remained inactive amid all this tumult; but the instant its master ceased to sound, it stamped with impatience, and strained every nerve to overtake its fellows.

Chapter 5

THE BATTLE OF MEDELLIN (MERIDA)

About the middle of February, our *corps d' armée* left La Mancha; and the troops under the command of General Sebastiani, the successor of Marshal Lefevre, came to the neighbourhood of Toledo, to watch the fragments of the army of the Duke de l'Infantado. We proceeded to occupy the towns of Talavera, Arzobispo and Almarez, on the right bank of the Tagus, confronting the Spanish army of Estremadura. This army had been dispersed on the 24th December by Marshal Lefevre at Arzobispo opposite Almarez, but had since been reorganized and recruited under the command of General Cuesta. It had recovered the bridge of Almarez from the French; and blown up the principal arches, which completely arrested the march of our troops, and obliged us to erect a new bridge over the Tagus, under the very fire of the enemy. We had indeed the possession of two other bridges, the one at Arzobispo, and the other at Talavera; but the route by these was at that time impracticable for artillery. Marshal Victor fixed his head-quarters at Almarez, that he might the better protect the works, and oversee the construction of the floats. Part of our division of light cavalry crossed the left bank of the river, to watch the enemy, and reconnoitre their right flank on the Ibor.

On account of the scarcity of forage and other necessaries, we were obliged to change our cantonments frequently. Almost the whole country occupied by our troops had been abandoned by its inhabitants. Before going, they used to brick up, in a secret place of their dwellings, every thing of value which they could not remove. The first thing, therefore, our soldiers did in coming to their empty and unfurnished houses, was to measure like architects the outside wails, and then the inside rooms, to examine if any space had been taken off. Sometimes we also found vessels of wine concealed in the earth. We were thus taught to live on chance-offerings, passing whole weeks without a supply of bread, and without being able to procure barley for our horses.

On the 14th of March, our floats were at length finished; but we could neither launch them, nor construct a bridge, under the fire of the enemy. It was therefore found necessary to dislodge them from the strong position they held before Almarez, at the confluence of the Ibor and the Tagus. On the 15th of March, part of the first *corps d' armée* crossed the Tagus at Talavera and Arzobispo, to bear upon the flank and rear of the Spaniards. General Laval's German Division first attacked the enemy on the morning of the 17th, at the village of Messa de Ibor. With the bayonet alone, and without artillery, 3000 men of that division routed 8000 Spaniards, who were intrenched on a lofty eminence, and fortified with six pieces of cannon. The 18th was spent in driving the enemy from Valdecannar, and chasing them from one place to another, and from rock to rock, as far as the defile of Miravette. Our regiment formed part of the left wing of the army, along with Vilatte's division. We moved upstream of the Ibor, easily repulsing the Spaniards who retained not a single post whenever they saw it assaulted.

The 19th, being occupied with the launch of the bridge floats, the army made no advance. The portable bridge being completed before night, the troops that remained on the right bank of the Tagus, and the artillery, began to pass over immediately. By the 20th, the whole army was united again at Truxillo. A little before our arrival, there had been an action before that city between the 5th Chasseurs à Cheval, which formed our advanced guard, and the Royal Carabineers of the enemy's rear guard. The number killed on either side was nearly equal, but the Spaniards lost the commander of a squadron.

The night was passed by both armies in sight of each other; and an hour before sunrise next morning, the enemy were on their march. We followed them soon after. The 10th Chasseurs à Cheval formed the advanced guard of our division of light cavalry, which cleared the way itself for all the troops. Four companies of light infantry passed on before us, when we came to a district intersected with forests and hills. Two hours before sunset, our vanguard squadron of Chasseurs came up with the rear guard of the enemy, which, being closely pressed, soon retired on the main body. The Colonel of the 10th Chasseurs à Cheval, driven by a rash bravery, permitted the whole regiment to make a charge, which soon began, and they pursued the Spanish cavalry for more than a league, on a causeway between craggy hills and river banks.

When a regiment or squadron of cavalry charges, either in line or column, the exact order in which it commenced to gallop cannot long be preserved; for the horses excite each other, and their ardour increases, till he who is best mounted finds himself foremost, and the line of battle is broken. The leader of an advanced party ought always to be cautious never to charge but for a very short distance, and to rally his men often, that the horses may recover their wind, and there be time to guard against a surprise. Besides, in all cases where a troop is too far in advance to be instantly assisted by another corps, there ought to be a reserve of at least one half of the company to sustain the other, and afford a kind of defence to those who are attacked, behind which they may again form, if they are repelled and pursued by a superior force.

Near the village of Miajadas, the Spaniards stationed an ambuscade of several squadrons of their best cavalry, which fell suddenly on our Chasseurs of the advanced guard, who were riding scattered and disorderly, the one before the other. Our Chasseurs were overpowered by numbers; their horses, exhausted with a most unmeasured charge, could not unite for their defence; and in less than ten minutes the enemy had disabled more than 150 of the bravest of the troop.

General Lasalle being apprised of what was passing, sent us instantly to their relief. We arrived too late, seeing only the distant trace of the Spaniards in the dust they raised in retiring. The colonel of the 10th Chasseurs à Cheval was intent in again drawing up his men, who were tearing their hair out with vexation, and assisting their wounded comrades to rise that were strewed all around. As the night was coming on, we returned to bivouack in the rear of the scene of action. At every step we encountered such of the wounded as had not yet received succour. Seeing us pass, they cried out, "*Comrades à moi, ne abandonnez pas*"—"Comrades, do not abandon us." We assisted them to mount our own horses, but some of them again fell to the ground, and expired in the arms of their fellow-soldiers.

On the 22nd of March the enemy crossed the River Guadiana. We occupied separate quarters in the environs of Miajadas and San Pedro. Our artillery at length arriving on the 23rd, the greater part of the army was concentrated in and around the city of Merida.

During the night of the 27th, the whole army was

in motion to march against the enemy. For several days General Cuesta had waited for us in the plains before Medellin, having previously surveyed, with the help of engineers, the advantageous position where his army was stationed. The Spaniards, to whom pitched battles had proved so frequently unfavourable, sought by every method to gain that confidence which they so much needed. They regarded the skirmish at Miajadas as a sign of future success. They relied also on some ancient superstition associated with the remembrance of the conquests their ancestors had achieved over the Moors, in the very plains which are watered by the River Guadiana. The French disregarded their confidence, and trusted from habit in the certainty of victory.

After crossing the river, by a very long and narrow bridge, one enters the city of Medellin. Beyond it lies an extensive plain without plantations, which stretches up the River Guadiana between that river, the city of Don Benito, and the village of Mingabril. The Spaniards at first occupied the heights between these towns; and afterwards extending their line farther, they formed a sort of crescent, with the left at Mingabril, their centre before Don Benito, and the right wing near the River Guadiana.

At eleven in the morning, we marched out from Medellin to draw up in order of battle. A short way from the town, we formed into the arc of a very compact circle, between the River Guadiana and a ravine planted with trees and vineyards, which stretches from Medellin to Mingabril. General Lasalle's division of light cavalry was stationed on the left, the German legion of infantry in the centre, and the Dragoons of General Latour Maubourg on the right. The divisions of Vilatte and Ruffin formed the reserve. Numerous detachments, from the three divisions which composed the first line, had been left in the rear of the army, to preserve our communications; and their strength did not exceed 7000 soldiers. The enemy before us presented an immense line of more than 34,000 men.

The German Legion began the attack. The 2nd and 4th regiments of Dragoons having next made a charge against the Spanish infantry, were repulsed with loss, and the German Division remained alone in the middle of the fight. They formed into a square, and courageously withstood the redoubled fury of the enemy as long as the action continued. With much difficulty, Marshal Victor renewed the combat, by causing two regiments of Vilatte's division to advance. The enemy's cavalry at first endeavoured to carry our right wing, but without success. Part of them then rushed *en masse* on our left, which, afraid of being surrounded, was forced to fall back on the River Guadiana, where it makes an angle, and contracts the plain towards Medellin. For two hours we retired slowly and quietly, facing about every fifty paces to present our front to the enemy, and to dispute our ground with them before yielding it, when they attempted to seize it by force.

Amid the endless whining of bullets flying over our heads, and the deafening roar of bomb-shells rending the air, and tearing up the earth around us, we heeded only the voice of our commanders. They gave their orders with the greater coolness and deliberation, the fiercer grew the enemy's attack. The farther we retired, the louder shouted our foes. Their sharpshooters were so numerous and daring, that they sometimes compelled our own Voltigeurs to fall into the ranks. They called to us at a distance, in their own language, that no quarter would be given, and that the plains of Medellin would be the tomb of the French. If our squadron had given way and fled, the cavalry of the Spanish right would have assaulted the rear of our army through the breach, and surrounded it completely. Then the field of Medellin would, indeed, have been our grave, as our enemies boasted.

General Lasalle rode backward and forward in front of his division, in a lofty and fearless manner. When the enemy's cavalry came within gun-shot, the sharpshooters of both sides retired. In the space which separated us, there might then be seen the horses of dead friends and foes, running on every side, most of them wounded, some of them dragging their masters under their feet, and struggling to free themselves of the unmanageable load.

The Spaniards had sent against our single squadron six of their best, who advanced in close column with the Xeres Lancers at their head. This solid mass all at once began to trot, with the intention of charging us while we made our retreat. The captain of our squadron commanded his four platoons, which did not in all exceed 120 men, to wheel half round, at a walking pace, to the right. This being done, he straightened his line with as much self-possession as if no enemy had been near. The Spanish horse, struck with astonishment at his coolness, insensibly slackened their pace. The leader of the squadron took advantage of their surprise, and immediately gave the signal to charge.

Our Hussars, who had hitherto preserved, amid the incessant threats and abuses of the enemy, a deep unbroken silence, now drowned the shrill sound of the trumpet, as they dashed forward with one tremendous shout of joy and rage. The Spanish lancers, horror-struck, stopped short, and, turning round at half pistol-shot, overturned their own cavalry behind them. Terror so impaired their judgment, that they could not look at each other, but believed everyone to be their enemy. Our Hussars rushed impetuously among them, and hewed them down without opposition. We chased them to the rear of their army, when the trumpets sounded a recall, and we returned, to form our squadron once more in order of battle. A little while after our charge, all the Spanish cavalry of the right and left had completely abandoned the field.

Our Dragoons now drew up around their chosen companions, and, perceiving an irresolution in the enemy's infantry, on seeing the flight of their cavalry, we improved our advantage, and made a most brilliant and fortunate charge against the centre of their army. At the same time, two, regiments of Vilatte's division attacked with success the right of the enemy's infantry, near the heights of Mingabril. In an instant, the army opposed to us disappeared like clouds before the wind. The Spaniards threw away their weapons and fled. The cannonade closed, and every corps of our cavalry joined in the pursuit.

Our soldiers, who had lately been threatened with certain death, if they had been overpowered, and were enraged by five hours defence, at first gave no quarter. The infantry followed the cavalry at a distance, and despatched the wounded with their bayonets. The vengeance of our soldiers fell chiefly on such of the Spaniards as were without a military uniform.

The Hussars and Dragoons who had gone abroad to forage, soon returned, guarding whole columns of Spaniards, whom they intrusted to the foot-soldiers to take to Medellin. Those very men, who had denounced us for slaughter with such confidence before the battle, now marched with humble aspect, crouching in fear. At every threatening sign made by our soldiers, they ran together like sheep when chased by dogs, squeezing to get to the middle of the crowd. Every time they met a body of French troops, they exclaimed with vehemence, "*Desean Napoleon vivo y su ejército valiente!*"—"Long live Napoleon and his brave army!" Now and then a passing horseman would take a pleasure in exacting these acclamations for himself, which were due alone to the victors as a whole.

A certain colonel who was a courtier, and an aide-de-camp of King Joseph's, looking at the prisoners as they filed past the regiments, called to them in Spanish to shout a "*Vive*" for King Joseph. They seemed at first not to comprehend his meaning, but after a moment's silence, they raised their old cry, "Long live Napoleon and his brave army!" The colonel then turned to a particular prisoner, and enforced his order with threats. The Spaniard having exclaimed "*Viva Joseph!*" an officer, who, as usual, had not been disarmed, approached his country's soldier, and ran his sword through his body. Our enemies were willing enough to do homage to our bravery; but they would not, even in their humiliation, recognise the power of a master not of their own choice.

A little before night I returned to Medellin. Silence and peace had succeeded the turmoil of battle and the peals of victory. In the plain alone there might be heard the wailings of the wounded, and the low murmurings of the dying, who raised their heads before they breathed their last to pray to God and the Holy Virgin. Death had impressed on the countenances of the slain, the expression of the passions which animated them at the moment they expired. Those who had been struck down when flying, were lying on their breast or side, with drooping heads, and fear-contracted muscles. Those again who had died while fighting bravely, retained, even when fallen, the aspect of defiance. Two regiments of Swiss and Walloon guards were stretched on the ground in the very ranks in which they had fought. Broken ammunition-waggons and cannon abandoned by their teams of mules, still marked the position of the Spaniards. Here and there lay wounded horses, whose limbs being shattered by the bullets, they could not rise from the spot where they were doomed to perish. Ignorant of death, and unconscious of futurity, they browsed on the grass around them as far as they could reach.

The loss of the French did not exceed 4000. The Spaniards left 12,000 dead on the field of battle, and 19 pieces of artillery. We made 7000 or 8000 prisoners, but scarcely 2000 of these arrived at Madrid. The Spanish captive in his own country could easily effect his escape.

The inhabitants of the towns and villages assembled in great numbers in the way of the French escorts, and withdrew their attention from their charge. They took care to leave their doors open, and the prisoners, mixing with the crowd in passing, darted into the houses, whose doors were instantly shut. Our soldiers, whose humanity returned when the combat was over, turned a blind eye to their flight, notwithstanding the strictness of the orders they had received.

The Spanish prisoners would address some Grenadier of the Guard, and, pointing to some distant village, with a heavy sigh, would say in their own language, "*Senor Soldado*," &c. "Mr Soldier, that is our home; there are our wives and children; must we pass so near, and never see them again? Must we leave them all to go to far off France?" The grenadier, affecting to speak sternly, would reply, "I am commanded to shoot you if I perceive you attempt to run away, but I don't see behind me." He would then step a little forward, and the prisoners, taking to the fields, would soon rejoin their armies. We were at last obliged to escort our prisoners with soldiers from the German Legion, their national character, and a stricter discipline, rendering them more vigilant and inflexible.

Part of our regiment was quartered at Mingabril, on the very field where the battle bad been fought, and where it raged the hottest. We lived among carcasses, and often saw proceeding from them thick black vapours, which the winds bore away to spread contagion and disease through the surrounding country. The oxen of La Mesta, that usually winter on the banks of the River Guadiana, fled in panic from their pastures. Their mournful bellowings, and the endless howling of the dogs that watched them, defined the feeling of terror that afflicted them.

Thousands of huge vultures collected from all parts of Spain in that vast, lonely valley of death. Perched on the heights, and, seen far off between our position and the horizon, they seemed as large as men. Our videttes more than once marched towards them to reconnoitre, mistaking them for an enemy. These birds would not leave their human repast on our approach, until we came within a few yards of them; then the beating of their vast wings above our heads resounded far and near, like the funereal echoes of the tomb.

The day before the battle of Medellin, or Merida, a complete victory was obtained by General Sebastiani, near Ciudad Real, in La Mancha, over the Spanish army stationed to defend the defiles of the Sierra-Morena. This victory of Ciudad Real, along with that which we gained at Medellin, struck terror into the remotest corners of Andalusia, and for a while, every route through it remained open to the French.

Notwithstanding these two severe losses, the Spanish Government was not worried. Like the Roman Senate, which voted thanks to the consul Varro, after the defeat of Cannae, because he did not fear for the safety of Rome, the Supreme Junta of Seville decreed, that Cuesta and his army had merited the gratitude of Spain, and they adjudged them the same rewards as if they had been successful. To have censured Cuesta and his army, in the present desperate state of affairs, would have been to confess themselves conquered. Fifteen days after the action at Medellin, the Spanish army had retrieved all its losses, and had thrown itself between our march and the passes of the mountains, with a force nearly 30,000 strong.

General Sebastiani advanced no further in La Mancha than Santa Crux de la Mudella, and our corps cantoned between the Tagus and the River Guadiana. We could not move in advance of that river, without seeing numerous new levies of Spaniards immediately raised in our rear, and having our only communications with Madrid, by the bridge of Almarez, intercepted. Besides, we had heard nothing for a long time of Marshal Soult's army, which should have entered Portugal, and with which our right was to have joined with.

The French army in the north of the Iberian Peninsula did not meet with the same degree of success as we obtained by our superior discipline in the central plains of Estremadura and La Mancha. These troops, commanded by Marshal Soult and Ney, had to carry on a warfare in a mountainous region, where the activity, numbers, and local knowledge of the natives, could at any time enable them to elude all our tactics, and all the experience of our greatest leaders.

After the retreat of General Moore, and the capitulation of Corunna and Ferrol, in the month of January, Marshal Soult proceeded in the direction of Portugal by San Jago, Vigo, and Tuy. Finding it impossible to cross the Minho, near its mouth, under the fire of the Portuguese forts on the opposite bank, he went up the river to Orense, where he passed it on the 6th of March. He completely routed on the 7th, the army of the Marquis de la Romana on the heights of Orsuna, near Monte Rey, and compelled the remains of that force to take refuge among the high mountains of Puebla de Senabria.

Chaves, a frontier town of Portugal, was invested by him on the 13th, and surrendered by capitulation. He entered Braga on the 19th, after having forced the pass of Carvalho d'Esté, one of the strongest positions of Portugal. Oporto, defended by an intrenched camp and 270 cannon, was taken by storm on the 29th; and the advanced guard of his army passed the Douro, and marched for Vouga, forty-five leagues distant from Lisbon.

The French had scarcely entered Oporto victoriously, when the garrisons they had left behind to overawe the country, and preserve the communications, were every where seized. The Portuguese troops of the fortress of Caminha, situated at the mouth of the Minho, crossed that river on the 10th of March, and were reinforced by a great number of Spanish marines, and the inhabitants of the Galician shores, who had taken arms under the orders of their clergy. They fortified the bridge of San Payo against the French, who might come from San Jago; and forced the cities of Vigo and Tuy to capitulate, where Marshal Soult had left garrisons and the magazines and depots of his *corps d'armée*. The Portuguese general, Francisco Silveira, who on the first approach of the French, had retired to Villa-Pouca, made himself master also of Chaves, on the 21st of March. After this, he proceeded to Amarante on the Tamega, to guard that important station, and harass the French detachments and rear-guards in the neighbourhood of Oporto.

The Marquis de la Romana, on the 30th of March, descended from the mountains of Puebla de Sanabria with several thousand men, the fragments of his vanquished force. He marched to Ponteferrada, and made a few Frenchmen prisoners, found some ammunition and provisions, and seized a damaged twelve-pounder, which he repaired. He then crossed the Castile road, and, with the help of his single cannon, obtained possession of Villa-Franca, and made the garrison of 800 men prisoners of war. On the news of these trivial successes, his army increased like a snow-ball rolling down a mountain slope, growing larger as it rolls until it becomes a mighty avalanche. Romana obliged Marshal Ney to abandon Bierzo, and concentrate his troops at Lugo—he then threw himself into Asturias, and raised Galicia also in arms.

The two French corps of Galicia and Portugal, having thus had their communications destroyed, were now completely isolated, and separated from the rest of our troops. They could no longer aid each other, or co-operate to further the common design of the general operations of the war. Their strength was now spent in a succession of partial actions, which were of no advantage.

Every effort of Marshal Ney's to terrify Galicia to submission, was vain. Instead of being restrained by severity, their hatred against the French was more indignantly roused. Violent measures were answered with even more violent reprisals, which always happens where there is a spark of patriotism. Whole squadrons, whole battalions, were butchered by the peasants in a single night. Seven hundred French prisoners were drowned in the Minho all at once, by command of Don Pedro de Barrios, Governor of Galicia, for the Junta. Instead of diminishing with our weakness, the rage of the people became daily more inflamed.

The inhabitants of Portugal, as well as those of Galicia, had universally risen in arms. They opposed the French with 70,000 militia, and 12,000 regular troops. It was impossible for Marshal Soult to keep the country in subjection behind him, and advance against Lisbon with only 22,000 men. Still, for more than forty days he remained in Oporto, vainly endeavouring to re-establish his interrupted correspondence. For months, he had received neither orders nor reinforcements; and he dared not make a retrograde movement, for fear of prejudicing the operations of other corps of our army, regarding whose positions he knew nothing. On the 2nd of May, he at length determined that the bridge of Amarante, on the Tamega should be seized by General Loison's division, in order to depart from Portugal by the route of Braganza.

Whilst this enterprise was going on, the French picquets on the Vouga were attacked by the English on the 10th of May, and they crossed the Douro the day following. The English, who had returned to Portugal after the retreat of Sir John Moore, were reduced to 15,000 men; and they dared not at first land their heavy baggage and artillery, but kept themselves ready to embark again on the first approach of the French. On the 4th, and again on the 22nd of April, they had received considerable reinforcements; and they advanced against Oporto with a force upwards of 23,000 strong.

The French quitted that city on the 12th of May, and their rear guard had a skirmish with the vanguard of the English army. Marshal Soult was pursued, and encircled by a triple army; the first, commanded by General Sir Arthur Wellesley, never lost sight of his rear; the second was the Anglo-Portuguese army, under General Beresford, which took the direction of Chaves, by Lamega and Amarante, keeping up with the Marshal's right; the third was commanded by the Portuguese General, Francisco Silveira, which preceded the other two, to cut off the French from the passes of Ruivaes, between Salamonde and Montalègre.

Marshal Soult, finding the route by Chaves occupied by Marshal Beresford, rapidly concentrated his army on Braga, and directed his march by the mountain road for Orense. He crossed sixty leagues of an insurgent territory, without sustaining any other very material loss than his heavy baggage and artillery, which he lost among ways that were impassable. The English advanced no further than Montalègre, but returned immediately towards the Tagus, and the neighbourhood of Lisbon.

Marshal Soult arrived at Lugo in Galicia on the 22nd of May, relieved the garrison of this town, which the Spaniards had besieged, and opened a communication with Marshal Ney, who was returned from an expedition against Oviedo, in the Asturias. A few days afterwards he resumed the offensive, against the army of the Marquis de la Romana, and followed it by Monforte, Ponteferrada, Bollo, and Viana; but it eluded his pursuit. Leaving Galicia, he then proceeded to Zamora by Puebla de Sanabria, for the purpose of following the movement of the English army, who appeared to be moving towards the Tagus in Estremadura, against Marshal Victor's corps.

Marshal Ney was obliged to retire into the kingdom of Leon, after Marshal Soult had departed. He had been unable to make any permanent footing in Galicia and the Asturias, having been constantly prevented by the villagers, and numerous peasant armies, whose strength daily increased, and could not be subdued.

In those mountainous provinces of the north of the Peninsula, though the French never failed to conquer in pitched battles with their enemies, they were, nevertheless, assailed incessantly by bands of armed mountain guerillas; who, without venturing to engage in close array, or corps against corps, always retired from rock to rock, and from one position to another among the heights, firing perpetually even while moving.

It was often necessary to send a whole battalion to carry orders to another near at hand. The wounded, the exhausted, or the diseased French soldier, who fell behind his column for a moment, was soon killed. After one battle was gained, we required to commence another conflict immediately. The persevering invincible spirit of the Spaniards, rendered our victories valueless. The French armies melted away for want of rest, amid their constant toils, watchings, and distresses.

Such are the events that had passed in the north of Spain, and prevented our *corps d'armée* of Estremadura and La Mancha, from profiting by their signal victories of Medellin and Ciudad Real. The army of Arragon had also been obliged to suspend its operations, by the French being necessitated to recall from that province the corps of Marshal Victor to Valladolid, to carry succours to Marshal Ney, and re-establish a line of communication in Galicia.

The French army in Spain had received no reinforcements to recruit its daily losses, since the campaign of Austria, and the departure of the Emperor Napoleon. Instead of being concentrated, it had, under the command of King Joseph, continued to spread itself more every day throughout the Peninsula. Weak on all points, because we were too much dispersed, we were enfeebled even by our conquests. In contending with the insurgent peasants of Galicia, of Portugal, and of the Asturias, we had lost that character of invincibleness, which was even more mighty than the actual force by which we had conquered so many countries.

King Joseph had acted as commander-in-chief since the departure of the Emperor. He believed that he could in Spain, as well as in Naples, by the well-known mildness of his temper, attach the people to his new sceptre, whom the power of our arms had subdued. He had allowed the French armies to advance every where in the Peninsula, for the sole end of organizing new provinces, and extending his sway over a greater extent of territory. Thus he had bartered away the military strength of the armies of Galicia and Portugal, concerning whom we knew nothing, for five whole months.

King Joseph had contracted indolent habits on the peaceful throne of Naples. Surrounded by flatterers, and some beguiling Spaniards, he resigned himself to foolish hopes. In place of attending to the army, he remained in his capital, immersed in effeminacy, and sighing after the luxuries of Italy. He wished to reign and sleep at Madrid, as he had done at Naples, even before we had won for him, if that were possible, a kingdom at the hazard of our lives.

He filled the columns of his Gazettes with decrees that were never enforced, and were scarcely ever read. He bestowed on one church the wax and consecrated vessels of another, long ago plundered by the French, or despoiled by the Spaniards themselves. He was prodigal in bestowing the decorations of his Royal order on his courtiers, who dared not wear them beyond the precincts of those places we occupied, for fear of being assassinated by the peasants of Spain. He made several promotions in his Royal army, which had not yet a being. He gave, in expectation, the places of governors, administrators, and judges, in the remotest provinces of his kingdom in both hemispheres; while he durst not sleep in any of his country-houses only a few leagues out of Madrid. He pulled down old houses, as his brother had done at Paris, intending to embellish his capital; but he wanted money to erect the new edifices, and his liberality extended no further than removing the rubbish.

To conciliate the people, he studied to imitate his predecessors Charles IV., and Ferdinand VII., by all possible methods, in their ostentatious pomp, their formality, and even their trifling sanctity. He walked himself with the processions in the streets of Madrid, and made the officers of his staff and the soldiers of his body-guard follow him, carrying lighted tapers. All this assumed piety, this affectation of munificence, this hypocritical liberality, had no other effect but to make him be ridiculed, when the terror, which ennobled all, was dissipated after the departure of the Emperor.

The Spaniards took delight in spreading a report, that King Joseph was addicted to drunkenness, and that he was blind of an eye. This story made a deep impression on the minds of the country people, although nothing could be more unfounded. It was in vain that he endeavoured to destroy these prejudices, by showing himself frequently in public, and looking everyone full in the face. The people, nevertheless, believed that he had but one eye.

On the day of his coronation, all ranks were admitted *gratis* to the places of public amusement, and, at one of the theatres, a farce was exhibited, called *Harlequin, Emperor of the Moon*. Several times during the representations of the piece, the people openly applied passages of it to the ephemeral condition of King Joseph at Madrid. Devotees, who were accustomed to using in their conversation *"Jesus, Maria, y Joseph"*, would stop short after repeating the first two names, and, after a pause, would adopt the circumlocutory, *"y el Padre de nuestor Senior"*—"and the Father of our Lord." They were afraid lest they would bring down blessings on King Joseph, by naming him who was regarded as his patron saint in heaven.

The good-nature of King Joseph came at last, by the French themselves, to be reckoned a defect. His ardent desire to make himself beloved by his new subjects, did real detriment to the success of military operations. The Spaniards had always the right, and the French the wrong side, in any case of complaint. We were frequently without food in districts that had submitted for the moment;

not daring to exact there, as from enemies, the provisions we required. Our soldiers expired by hundreds, in the hospitals of Burgos and Madrid, in want of the most necessary articles.

After successful engagements, he would go to the *Retiro* to swear in the prisoners sent thither by the army, and declare to them that they had been misled by villains, and that he, their King, desired only their welfare, and their country's happiness. The prisoners, expecting to be shot before night, would first take the oath of fidelity he exacted; and, when armed and accoutred, they would then desert, and return to their armies. This made our soldiers term King Joseph "The principal administrator and organizer general of the military depots of the Supreme Junta of Seville."

The French Generals and Marshals were unwilling to obey a man whom they could not recognise as a Frenchman, now that he was acknowledged King of Spain. They even often tried to contradict and displease him, that they might be remanded back to Germany. They wished to abandon this irregular war, which was both unpopular with the army, and deprived them of the chance of being distinguished, or obtaining higher promotion, by fighting under the eye of the Emperor. The Spanish war was impoverishing France, without kindling the military enthusiasm of the nation.

King Joseph had neither sufficient authority or military genius, nor enough of self-confidence to direct the operations, which the unforeseen changes of general affairs rendered indispensably necessary. He dared not issue any orders, without consulting his brother. The plans came all from Paris or Germany; sometimes they arrived too late, and at best they could only be imperfectly executed, by one who had no share in their formation. The French army in Spain was totally devoid of that unity of action, without which the simplest operations of war cannot prosper.

In the month of April, the corps of Marshal Victor, to which we belonged, left for a time its cantonments on the River Guadiana, between Merida and Medellin; and approached the Tagus and Alcantara, to unite with the division of Lapisse, which had proposed terms of surrender to Ciudad Rodrigo, but without effect. A division of the Marshal's corps crossed that river on the 14th of May, after a slight engagement with the Portuguese militia, and proceeded once more to Alcantara. The 8th was spent reconnoitring in the direction of Castel. Blanco; but having learned that 8000 English and Portuguese were in possession of Abrantes, they conjectured that Marshal Soult's expedition against Lisbon had failed, and therefore they returned. Marshal Victor then collected together his troops in the vicinity of Truxillo, between the River Guadiana and the Tagus, to secure his communications by the bridge of Almarez, to cover Madrid, and observe the army of Cuesta. The fourth corps, commanded by General Sebastiani, had continued in La Mancha since the engagement at Ciudad-Real.

On the 20th of May, the officers and subalterns of the fourth squadron of all the cavalry regiments in the army, received orders from the Minister of War to return to the head depots of their regiments, in order to raise additional squadrons. In consequence of this appointment, I quitted Spain, and on my arrival in France, was sent against the English on the coast of Flanders. Their expedition against the fleet and dockyards at Antwerp having failed, through the slowness and indecision of their leader, I returned to Spain at the commencement of the following year.

Chapter 6

THE BATTLE OF TALAVERA

After Marshal Soult had been obliged to leave Oporto and Portugal, the English army again passed the Douro, and returned to the towns of Thomar and Abrantes, near the Tagus, intending to march against Spanish Estremadura, by way of Coria and Placencia. The corps of Marshal Victor, occupying the country around Truxillo and Caceres, being apprehensive that the English would get behind them by the right bank of the Tagus, crossed that river in the beginning of June, and retired to Calzada, and afterwards on the 26th, to Talavera de la Reyna.

On the 20th of July, the English army, commanded by General Sir Arthur Wellesley, formed a junction at Oropeza with the Spanish army of General Cuesta. The number of the English was about 20,000, with from 4000 to 5000 Portuguese. General Cuestas army amounted to 38,000. Another Spanish army, under the command of General Venegas, of 18,000 or 20,000 men, waited to co-operate with General Sir Arthur Wellesley and Cuesta, in La Mancha.

A party of Portuguese and Spaniards of the advance, commanded by the English General Wilson, passed on to Escalona by the Arenas mountains, arriving on the 23rd, so as to open a communication with the Spanish army of General Venegas, which was advancing from Tembleque by Ocana, to Aranjuez and Valdemoro. Generals Wilson and Venegas were to march upon Madrid, and endeavour to get possession of with the co-operation of the inhabitants. This combined movement was intended to oblige King Joseph to concern himself solely with the safety of his capital, and to prevent him from concentrating his scattered forces. The Anglo-Spanish armies hoped soon to overcome the French, or at least to expel them from Madrid and the centre of Spain, and force them to cross the mountains and retire to Segovia.

The armies of Generals Wellesley and Cuesta, advanced on the 22nd of July to Talavera. Not far from that city, the cavalry of General Cuesta gained a slight advantage over the rear-guard of the French cavalry, which withdrew to the main body. This success inspired the Spaniards with the most confident hopes, longing to avenge their defeat at Medellin by attacking the French themselves, whom they believed to be half-defeated because they had retired. They left the English at Talavera, and unwisely advanced by El Bravo and Santa Olalla, towards Torrijos.

Marshal Victor retired behind the Guadarama, near to Toledo, and on the 25th was joined by the corps of General Sebastiani, and the troops brought from Madrid by King Joseph. The whole central French army thus united amounted to 47,000 men, and on the 26th it marched for Talavera, under the command of King Joseph.

The 2nd regiment of Hussars, which formed part of the French advanced guard, almost annihilated Villa Viciosas regiment of Dragoons, in the defile of Alcabon, near to Torrijos, and the whole army of Cuesta retired precipitately behind the Alberche. The French crossed the river in the afternoon of the following day, drove in the English picquets, and arrived by five o'clock within cannon-shot of the enemy.

The Spaniards were posted in a situation deemed impregnable, behind old walls and garden fences, which border and encompass the city of Talavera. Their right was defended by the Tagus, and their left joined the English, near a redoubt constructed on an eminence. The ground in front of the Anglo-Spanish armies was very unequal, and intersected here and there by ravines, formed by the rains of winter. The whole extent of their position was covered by the channel of a pretty deep torrent, at that time dry. The English left was strengthened by a conical hill that commanded the greater part of the field of battle, and which was separated by a deep and extensive valley from the Castilian mountain range.

This eminence was, in a way, the key to the enemy's position and against this decisive point of attack, an experienced general, possessed of that intuitive intelligence which insures success, would immediately have led the principal part of his available force, to obtain possession of it. He would either have taken it by assault, or have turned it by a flanking manoeuvre in the valley. But King Joseph, when he should have acted, was indecisive and uncertain. He attempted only half measures, he distributed his forces partially, and lost the opportunity of conquering his enemy by being too wary. Marshal Jourdan, the second in command, had not that spur of patriotism in the Spanish war, which inspired him when he fought in the plains of Fleurus, to achieve the independence of France, so he did not push his advice or military proposals strongly.

The French army commenced the engagement with a cannonade and rifle fire in advance of their right; and they despatched a single battalion only, with some skirmishing sharpshooters, by way of the valley, to take the hill which defended the English left flank, never thinking they would do otherwise than yield. This battalion, however, having to contend with superior numbers, was repulsed with considerable loss, and compelled to return. A small force of Dragoons, which had gone to reconnoitre Talavera, found the approaches to that city strongly fortified with artillery, and could not advance.

At nightfall, the French made another attempt to gain the hill. A regiment of infantry, followed at a short distance by two others, attacked the extreme left of the English army with unparalleled courage, arrived at the summit of the hill, and took possession of it. But having been fiercely attacked, in its turn, by the English, just having conquered, it, was breathless with exertion, it was immediately obliged to fall back. One of the two regiments commanded to assist in this attack, had lost its way, in a wood, on account of the darkness; the other not getting soon enough over the ravine, which covered the enemys position, had not arrived in time.

Both these attacks had miscarried, though conducted with intrepid bravery, because they had been made by an inadequate number of troops. A single battalion had been sent, when, instead, a great proportion of the whole army should have been despatched. These unsuccessful attempts revealed to the English what we intended to do the next day; and still more evidently demonstrated the importance of the station they held. They passed the greater part of the night in fortifying the hill with artillery.

The sun rose next morning on the two armies, drawn up in battle-order, and again the cannonade commenced. The defence of Portugal being intrusted to the English army, the fate of that country, and, perhaps, of all the Peninsula, was now to be decided by this contest. The veterans of the first and fourth French corps, for years succesful conquerors throughout Europe, brave, strong and well supported by the combined skill of their officers, burned with impatience for orders to engage, and were determined to overthrow the enemy by one well coordinated assault.

Only three regiments of infantry were sent by the valley to storm the position, which we had, for a moment, taken on the preceding evening. After considerable loss, they reached the top of the hill, and were nearly successful. One of the regiments had advanced as far as the artillery, when our charge was repulsed, and the three regiments were forced to retire. The English, realising by this renewed attack, that the French intended to turn their left by the valley, stationed their cavalry there; and caused the Spanish force to occupy the slopes of the high Castilian mountains beyond it. The French withdrew to the ground they first occupied. The cannonade continued for another hour, and then became gradually silent. The overpowering heat of mid-day obliged both armies to suspend the combat, and observe an involuntary truce, during which the wounded were removed.

King Joseph, having at last gone to reconnoitre the enemys position for himself, gave orders, at four o'clock, for a general attack against the English army. A brigade of Dragoons was left to observe the Spaniards in the direction of Talavera. General Sebastiani's corps marched against the right of the English, whilst Marshal Victor's infantry, followed by masses of cavalry, charged against their left, to attack the hill from the direction of the valley. King Joseph and Marshal Jourdan took post with the reserve, in the rear of the 4th division. The sound of artillery and musket fire were not long in being heard.

The English commander, stationed on the hill which overlooked the field of battle, was always present wherever danger called. He could survey, at a glance, every corps of his army, and perceive below him the least movement of the French forces. He saw the line of battle formed, the columns placed for the conflict; he deduced their designs by their arrangements, and thus had time to make his plans, so as to anticipate and foil those of his foes. The position of the English army was naturally strong and difficult to approach, both in front and flank; but in the rear it was quite accessible, and gave ample freedom to their troops to hasten to the quarter threatened.

The French had a ravine to pass before they could reach the enemy. They had to advance over ground much intersected, very rugged and uneven, obliging them frequently to break their line—and the positions of the line they attacked had been well fortified. The left could not see the right, or know what was passing there, because of the rising ground between them. Every corps of the army fought apart, with unparalleled bravery, and ability too; but there was no coordination of their efforts. The French were not then commanded by a senior general, whose knowledge and experience might have compensated for the difficult terrain.

The force of Lapisse first passed the ravine, attacked the fortified hill, ascended it in defiance of a fire of grapeshot, which mowed down its ranks, but was repulsed with the loss of its General, and a great number of officers and soldiers. In retreating, it left the right of the fourth corps uncovered, which the British artillery took in flank, and forced for a moment to retire. The left of General Sebastiani's corps, advanced under a most intense fire of artillery, to the foot of a redoubt on the right of the English force, and between the combined armies. The French attack was too far advanced, and too soon forward—it was intercepted and driven back by the united corps of the English right and the Spanish left. Assistance came, and the combat was renewed. In the centre, Marshal Victor rallied the force of

Lapisse at the foot of the hill, and abandoned all further attempt to gain possession of it. The French then tried to turn it either by the right or left flank. Vilattes troops advanced in the valley, and Ruffins moved to the right of this by the foot of the Castilian mountains. The cavalry, forming a second line were ready to march out onto the plain in the rear of the enemy, where the infantry could open a passage.

The English cavalry made a charge against the massed ranks of the French just as they began to move. They engaged in the valley, passed onwards, regardless of the fire of several battalions of our infantry, between the divisions of Vilatte and Ruffin, and fell with an impetuosity never surpassed on the 10th and 26th regiments of our Chasseurs á Cheval. The 10th could not resist the charge. They opened their ranks, but rallied immediately, and nearly the whole of the 23rd regiment of Light Dragoons, the foremost of the English cavalry, was either destroyed or taken captive.

The English Foot Guards, stationed on the left and centre of their army, being charged by the French, at first repulsed them vigorously; but one of its regiments being too far advanced, was in its turn taken in flank by the fire of the French artillery and infantry, sustained considerable loss, and retreated with some difficulty behind their second line.

The French took advantage of this success; they again moved forward, and but one other effort was necessary to break through onto the plain, and do battle on equal ground. But King Joseph thought it was too late to advance with the reserve, and the attack was delayed till the following day. Night again closed over us, and the conflict ceased from exhaustion, without either side having won such a decided advantage as to entitle it to claim the victory.

The corps of Marshals Victor and Sebastiani withdrew successively during the night towards the reserve, leaving an advanced guard of cavalry on the scene of the engagement, to take care of the wounded. The English, who expected a new attack in the morning, were greatly surprised, when day dawned, to see that their enemies, leaving twenty pieces of cannon, had retreated to their old position on the Alberche. The English and Spaniards, according to their own accounts, lost 6,616 men. The French had nearly 10,000 slain.

King Joseph left the first corps *d'armée* on the Alberche, and went with the fourth corps and the reserve to reinforce Toledo. That city, having a garrison of only 1,500 men, had been attacked by a division of the Spanish army of General Venegas, who had taken Aranjuez and Valdemoro on the 27th. Some days previously Madrid had nearly been seized by the vanguard corps of the English General Wilson, who had advanced from Escalona to Naval-Carnero. The inhabitants of the capital had opened their gates, and gone in crowds to meet him in their holiday dresses, after having obliged three French battalions, that formed the garrison, to shut themselves up in the fort of the *Retiro*. King Joseph strongly reinforced Toledo, and came on the 1st of August to Illescas, that he might be equally able in that situation to march against the army of Venegas, to assist the corps on the Alberche, and to subdue the inhabitants of Madrid.

The English retired on the 3rd of August to Oropesa, without attempting any attack against Marshal Victor. They left the Spaniards at Talavera, and General Wilsons corps at Escalona. On the night of the 4th, the combined English and Spanish armies suddenly passed the Tagus, by the bridge of Arzobispo, on the approach of the corps of Marshal Soult, Ney, and Mortier, who were advancing from Salamanca by Puerto de Banos, Placencia, and Naval-Moral, placing themselves between the English and the bridge of Almarez.

The advanced corps of Marshal Mortier crossed the Tagus on the 8th of August, at a ford below the bridge of Arzobispo, during the time of siesta, an hour after midday. They surprised part of the army of Cuesta, and captured his cannon, as well as those placed to defend the bridge. On the 11th, General Sebastiani defeated the army of Venegas at Almonacid, in La Mancha. The Spanish and Portuguese corps under General Wilson were completely routed on the 12th of August, near the mountains of Banos, by part of the force under Marshal Ney, who was falling back on Salamanca.

The expedition of General Sir Arthur Wellesley in Estremadura, was at least as hazardous as that attempted by General Moore at the close of the preceding year, against the corps of Marshal Soult at Saldanna. The whole English and Spanish armies would have fallen into the power of the French, if the corps of Marshals Soult, Ney and Mortier, had arrived one day earlier in Estremadura. But King Joseph did not venture to dispose of these troops, without having previously received authority from the Emperor Napoleon. He had only sent the order to Marshal Soult on the 22nd, to concentrate at Salamanca. This order was not received till the 27th. On the 28th he was on his march; but notwithstanding all his expedition, he only reached Placencia on the 3rd of August.

The English and Spanish armies remained behind the Tagus till the 20th of August, occupying Messa de Ibor, Deleytosa, and Jeraicejo, opposite Almarez. The bridge of boats there had been broken down by the Spaniards. They then retired towards the River Guadiana, and the army of Sir Arthur Wellesley re-entered Portugal.

The invasion of Estremadura by the English had caused the French to summon to the aid of the central army strong reinforcements, appointed to guard and defend the northern provinces of Spain; their combined strength was considerable. After the departure of the English, the Spanish government still persisted in the plan of fighting in great bodies. They assembled an army of 55,000 men in the plains of La Mancha, and that army was totally beaten and dispersed on the 10th of November at Ocana, by Marshal Mortiers forces, about 24,000 strong. The French had no difficulty in defeating troops hastily raised and undisciplined, who had no skill to manoeuvre, and embarrassed themselves by their very numbers, which should have been their strength.

The French ought to have again brought together all their disposable forces after the battle of Ocana, and instantly marched against Lisbon. But they passed the Sierra-Morena, and invaded nearly all Andalusia, except the Isle of Leon and Cadiz, without meeting a single opponent. In thus extending to the south of Spain, they gave the English time to fortify Portugal, and to gather the military strength of that kingdom. The French were weakened, by the army being again divided, being compelled to occupy and administer vast areas of the country. The Spaniards had everywhere an opportunity of again carrying on guerilla warfare, from which the French had suffered so much in the Asturias, in Galicia, and in the north of Portugal.

In consequence of the destruction of the Spanish armies, the Provincial Juntas, being unable to hold any communication with the Central Junta, devoted all their energies to the local defence of the districts under their administration. Such of the inhabitants as had hitherto endured with patience, waiting in the hope that regular warfare would bring them deliverance, now trusted solely to their own exertions, for the means of shaking off their galling yoke. Every province, every town, every individual, felt the necessity more and more keenly every day, of repulsing the French. The hatred against the French, which existed throughout Spain, had united the populace; and we now experienced, instead of regular warfare, a system of war in detail, a species of organized disorder, which exactly suited the unconquerable spirit of the Spanish nation, and their present wretched circumstances.

The districts of Spain occupied by the French were soon overrun by bands of partisans and guerillas, composed of the soldiers of dispersed armies, and the inhabitants of the plains and mountains. Clergymen, farmers, students, and simple shepherds, became active and enterprising leaders. Leaders like these, without military authority, without regular troops, could be, at first, only figureheads around whom the peasantry could by turns fight and rally. The report of any little success gained by these numerous parties, was greedily welcomed by the people, and spread with zeal and exaggeration. It elevated their spirits, which defeat in other quarters might for a moment have depressed. That very restlessness of imagination, and that spirit of independence, which had been of no help to the slow and undecided operations of the regular armies of the Junta, now became the popular cause. It might thus be said of the Spaniards, that if they were at first an easy prey to the French, to subdue them was an almost impossible task.

Whenever we moved from one province to another, the partisans of the enemy immediately commenced organizing the country in the name of Ferdinand VII, as if we had abandoned it entirely; and they then punished severely those of the inhabitants as had collaborated with the French. Thus the terrors of our army and weapons yielded us no advantage. As the enemy were spread throughout the whole country, the several points occupied by the French were all more or less threatened; our victorious troops, dispersed from Irun to Cadiz to control their conquests, were in a state of incessant blockade, and were, in fact, masters of the ground only on which they actually stood.

The garrisons, left to subdue the country, on the military roads, were continually attacked. They were obliged, for security, to construct small citadels, by repairing the old ruined castles on the heights. Sometimes these retreats were the remains of forts erected by the Romans or Moors, for the same purpose, many years ago. In the plains, our posts on the line of communication fortified one or two houses at the entry of the villages, to enjoy peace during the night, or for protection when danger menaced. The sentinels dared not station themselves beyond the bounds of the enclosures, lest they should be attacked and assassinated. They therefore occupied some tower, or lookout built of planks erected beside the chimney, in order to observe all that passed in their vicinity. The French soldiers, enclosed in their little fortresses, heard at times the mirthful sounds of the guitar-musicians of their enemies, who, being always well received and entertained by the people, came frequently to pass the night in the neighbouring villages.

The French armies could not receive any provisions or ammunition unless under the escort of very strong detachments, which were always harassed, and often slain. These convoys were but feebly opposed in the plains, but they were obliged to fight their way bravely whenever they entered the mountains. The daily losses sustained by the French in some parts of Spain, while procuring supplies, and securing their communications, were not less than they would have experienced if they had been constantly engaged with an enemy able to oppose them in the field.

The people of Spain did not give way to despondency, on account of the continuance of the war. In some provinces, the peasants were always armed; farmers held the plough with one hand, and a weapon in the other, always at the ready. This he buried in the ground, when the French approached in numbers too strong to promise victory. Their animosity increased with every new oppression to which they were exposed by the French. The evils patiently submitted to by other nations, because they are viewed as the inevitable consequences of war, were never failed to cause irritation and hatred to the people of Spain.

They employed by turns the greatest energy, or the most profound cunning, to satisfy their passionate resentments, when they felt they were the weaker party. Like vindictive vultures pursuing their prey, they followed after the French columns, to sacrifice such of the soldiers as fell behind on the march, from fatigue or from their wounds. Sometimes, also, the French soldiers, on their arrival in a place, were invited to feasts; the Spaniards plied them with wine to intoxicate them, so that they might be lulled into a false sense of security many thousand times more dangerous than the hazards of war. Then they called their partisans, and pointed out to them at night the houses where our soldiers were.

When other French soldiers went to avenge the deaths of their comrades, the inhabitants were gone, and they found nothing but deserted dwellings, on which they could not wreak their vengeance without punishing themselves, in destroying the houses of such villages, they would have been deprived of resources for the time to come.

When our detachments came in strength to the insurgent cities of Biscay or Navarre, the *Alcaids*, the women and the children, came around us as if war had been unknown, and the noise of forge-hammers pealed through the air. But we had no sooner departed, than all the labour ceased, and the people flew to arms, to harass our detachments among the rocks, and attack our rear guards. A war like this, on which the mind of the soldier had no fixed target against which to fight, repressed his courage, tired him and wore out his patience.

The French could only maintain possession of Spain through terror. They were always necessitated to punish the innocent with the guilty, and to avenge the offences of the powerful on the weak. Pillage had become an indispensable weapon in our armoury. The atrocities carried out against the hostile populace, and the injustice of the cause for which the French contended, destroyed the morale of the Spanish army, and sapped to the very core the foundations of military discipline, without which regular troops have neither power nor strength.

I returned to Spain about the end of the year 1809, bringing with me a detachment of eighty Hussars to my regiment. In the interior of France, one would have believed from the *Gazettes*, that the English, having retreated to Portugal after the battle at Talavera, waited only for a fair wind to embark—that the conquered country had a long while ago submitted to King Joseph—and that the French armies, at rest in good cantonments, had no other task but to wipe out some bands of brigands who pillaged and committed excesses on the peaceable inhabitants.

We joined several other detachments of light cavalry at Bayonne, and crossed the Bidassoa to sleep in Irun. Many of the inhabitants of all ages had assembled at the gates of that city to see us arrive, and followed after us for some time with evident curiosity. We thought at first that their reason for this attention, was to show their satisfaction at our arrival in their country. But we learned, when too late, that the people of Irun, as well as of other frontier towns, kept an exact account of all the French that entered Spain, and of all the wounded that left the country; and it was according to this information that the Spanish partisans and guerillas directed their operations.

All the detachments going, like ourselves, to reinforce the French army in Spain, received orders to rendezvous in the cities of Vittoria and Miranda, to be sent on an expedition against the Spanish partisans of Navarre and La Rioca. General Simon left Vittoria on the 13th of December with 1,200 men, and proceeded to occupy Salvatierra and Allegria. The commandants of the garrisons stationed in the cities of Navarre, had formed some flying columns, who were to join General Simon's forces, after having dispersed such parties of the enemy as they might fall in with on their march. This kind of military chase was designed to destroy the bands of the partisan Mina, who kept Pampeluna in a state of almost constant blockade, attacking without interruption the convoys going to the French army of Arragon.

Generals Loison and Solignac commenced their march on the 16th from Vittoria and Miranda, and, by a simultaneous movement on both sides of the Ebro, they threw themselves on Logrono, hoping to surprise the Marquis de Porliere in that city. The numerous guerillas of that partisan chief intercepted our communications between Bayonne and Madrid, making daily incursions even to the gates of Burgos, Bribiesca, Pancorvo, Miranda, and Vittoria.

My detachment of Hussars composed part of a corps of four or five thousand men, commanded by General Loison. The infantry had left their baggage behind them, and even their knapsacks, in order to be the more nimble for running among the mountains.

We came in sight of Logrono at four o'clock in the afternoon of the 17th. General Solignac's troops presented themselves before the city about the same time. They immediately took possession of all the gates and entrances on the right side of the Ebro, while we seized the bridge which leads to the left side of the river. We flattered ourselves, for an instant, that we had enclosed the partisans in Logrono; but, to our great surprise, we entered the city soon after, without needing to fire a single shot.

The Marquis de Porliere had been apprised in the morning of our combined march, and had escaped by the cross-roads to the high mountains of Castile. The inhabitants of the city, both men and women, stationed themselves at the windows to see us arrive. In general, their countenances displayed evident marks of contentment and satisfaction. They rejoiced that the Marquis of Porliere had avoided us, but truly not because they saw the French troops return. They knew full well, by past experience, that our coming would bring on them punishments for opposing our army.

General Solignac went off next day in search of the enemy. At Najara, he encountered a small party of Spaniards, whom he chased to La Clazada de Santo Domingo, thinking that he would reach the main body of the partisans. It was a stratagem of the Marquis de Porliere, intended to lead us in a direction opposite to that which he and his small army had taken. General Loison followed General Solignac on the 19th to Najara. We needed to halt two whole days in that city, to acquire some information about the enemy, whom we had completely lost.

On the 21st, we were at last informed, that the Marquis de Porliere had taken the road for Soto. This town, situated among the mountains, was the residence of a provincial Junta; and the magazine of their arms, ammunition and clothing, was also in this place. We ascended the Najarillo to pursue the partisans once more. General Loisons troops went to a village about ten leagues south of Soto, at the foot of high mountains, intending to spend the night there. A corps composed of my detachment of Hussars, one hundred and fifty Polish Lancers, and two hundred Voltigeurs, continued on to pursue the enemy. I cleared the march of this corps with an advanced guard of twenty-five Hussars. We pressed ahead through narrow, wretched roads, in the midst of snow, till sunrise, when we came up with the rear guard of the enemy, and took a few prisoners. We delayed several hours to feed our horses, and give General Loison time to arrive. At noon we resumed our march, on the left bank of a small river which flows towards Soto.

Some peasants were observed on the highest of the mountains towards our right, fleeing with their cattle. Small platoons of Spanish Cavalry, placed in watch on the heights, started off at the gallop as soon as they observed us. The clergy and *Alcaids* of the hamlets we passed through, with false friendship brought us refreshments on the way, evidently to hinder our advance. From fifty to sixty peasants, of all ages, whom I questioned in different places, all endeavoured to deceive me, by saying that they had not seen the guerillas, and that they were not at Soto. But horses, dying from fatigue, and abandoned on the road with their accoutrements, demonstrated at almost every step that we were not far distant from our foes.

As we came in sight of Soto, at about a quarter of a league off, we were suddenly met by a discharge from thirty or forty muskets; and some armed peasants were observed to flee from behind the rocks where they had been concealed, and to run down the mountains at full speed towards Soto. We halted, waiting for the infantry and the Major in command. No place could be found on the heights to form in battle-order, and we remained in file on the narrow path through which we had arrived.

Soto lies in the bottom of a narrow valley, which is divided by a torrent. On the other side of the town rises a very steep mountain, along the side of which there is a winding path. Up this road, we perceived the partisans in their flight exactly facing us. The magistrates of the Junta of Soto, and a great number of priests wrapped in black cloaks, marched foremost, and were near reaching the top of the mountain. The treasure and baggage followed next, borne by mules in files, the one tied behind the other. Then came the soldiers in uniforms, and a great many armed peasants, who marched without order. A crowd of all ages and sexes hurried tumultuously out of the town along with the partisans. The bustle of so many men, clambering up the mountains by different tracks, presented to the eye a truly strange appearance.

Confusion spread among the Spaniards on perceiving us, and at first they hastened their march by every path that was accessible. But, seeing that we were no more than a small advanced guard, they gathered courage, and the whole extent of the mountain resounded with their prolonged sonorous cries. Those who were nearest us stopped, and, stationing themselves on the rocks opposite, aimed at us with their muskets at their utmost stretch; and called out to us these words, ornamented with a thousand curses, "Come, look at the brigands a little nearer, if you dare!" It was thus our soldiers termed them, on account of their disorderly mode of fighting. They were separated from us by a ravine three or four hundred feet in depth, at the bottom of which the river flowed.

The Marquis de Porliere left behind him, to cover his retreat, a company of Cavalry before the gate of Soto, by which we had to enter. At a little distance on the other side of the river, he had posted four or five hundred infantrymen on the rocks and hills which overlooked the town. Whatever happened, these men could easily retreat without loss on our advance, but they could do us much harm.

The major of the 26th regiment, who commanded us, judging that the enemys position could not be carried in front, resolved to take it in flank. A hundred and fifty Voltigeurs descended the ravine, crossed the river at a ford below us, climbed the mountain with difficulty, and continued firing for some time at the enemy without gaining ground. Their ammunition failing them, they retired beside a small chapel on the top of the hill, and sent two men to tell us their condition. The firing, cursing, and shouting of the Spaniards, redoubled. They had observed our riflemen send for aid, and saw that we could not afford it.

The captain of the enemy's Cavalry advanced before his troop about half a gun-shot, near the entrance of the town, and began to provoke the officer who commanded the vanguard of our Hussars, by his abusive language. This captain made his horse prance, and fenced away with his sabre, to show that he could use it with dexterity. The Hussar officer at first regarded him with perfect indifference; but, rendered impatient by his bravado and the shouts of the Spaniards present, whose audacity was increasing, he descended the narrow winding path which leads to Soto unaccompanied. The warlike captain turned his horse's head when the officer was a few paces distant, and shrunk back quietly to the ranks of his Cavalry.

Now, however, the uneasiness of the Major was every moment increasing. General Loison had not arrived, daylight was fading, we heard more firing at the summit of the hill opposite, and we had received no news about our Voltigeurs.

When night arrived, we heard the Spanish drum beat a sort of retreat, and then we saw the flash of a pretty brisk fire of musketry at the bottom of the valley, between two parties who disputed the passage of the river. After the firing, a deep silence followed.

Solitude and night heightened our anxiety. We believed that our Voltigeurs had come down the mountain opposite, through the midst of the enemy, and that, overpowered by superior force, they had been beaten. The Major in command sent my detachment forward to render some assistance if possible. On entering the city, we met, instead of Spaniards, the division of General Loison entering in files. Led astray by their guides, they had taken a road quite different from us, and very circuitous. The engagement, which had appeared so bloody to us at a distance, was in fact between our Voltigeurs, who were descending to the town after the enemys departure, and the Grenadiers of General Loisons advanced guard. These friends arriving at the same time from opposite directions, did not recognise each other till after the second discharge. Fortunately, the darkness of the night prevented them from taking aim, and there was but one man killed on either side.

Soto was abandoned by its inhabitants. The air now resounded with the rough voices of the soldiers, who ran through the streets and burst open the doors of the houses, to find food and lodging. In the midst of this confused uproar, which the echoes of the adjoining mountains endlessly redoubled, we heard the cry of a distressed woman, who, in an unearthly voice, never ceased the whole night to cry for help. Having been left in the hospital of the town when the inhabitants fled, she had been terrified by the chaos she saw in the streets, through the bars of her grated window. Her voice was raised amid the tumult, as if she was the representative of the whole fugitive population.

A fire was soon after seen among the heights, and we heard the crash of falling walls. Then an explosion took place, and we saw the flaming wreck of a building blown into the air. The fire had reached some chests of cartridges which the enemy, unable to carry with them, had concealed beneath a quantity of straw. At sunrise, we left Soto, and for two days followed the track of the partisans in the direction of Munilla and Cervera. Despairing at last of being able to strike at them, we took up our quarters in the town of Arnedo, and then returned to Logrono.

General Simon had no better success in his expedition into Navarre against Mina. That guerilla leader, being attacked on the 19th at Estella, and on the 20th at Puente de la Reyna, disbanded his followers, and thus avoided the troops that were marching from every quarter against him. General Simon was no sooner gone, than Mina again collected his forces. The Marquis de Porliere, driven from the mountains of Castile, retraced his steps, and threw himself among those of Asturias. In this retreat, where he was pursued by a force at least four times stronger than his own, he did not lose more than thirty men.

By the accounts of the French commanders at this period, it appears that bands, similar to those of Porliere and Mina, existed in every province of Spain occupied by the French. These guerillas did incalculable damage to our armies, and no power could destroy them. Incessantly pursued, frequently dispersed, they always rallied again, and renewed their harassment of our army.

Chapter 7

ANDALUSIA

For nearly a month we remained in the province of La Rioca; afterwards, we marched for Burgos, to join our regiment in Andalusia. On the 25th of January we arrived at Madrid, and stayed five days in a village near that capital, waiting for a detachment of our regiment on its way from France, with baggage, money, and a fresh supply of horses.

This new detachment having arrived, an adjutant-major, under whose care it had been placed, took the command of our column of Hussars. We crossed to La Mancha, and soon after arrived at Santa Cruz, a small town at the foot of the Sierra Morena. These mountains, which separate La Mancha and Andalusia, are inhabited by some colonists from different parts of Germany, brought thither by Count Olivades in 1781. The most aged of these emigrants followed us on foot for hours, to enjoy once more, before their death, the happiness at talking in their native language with such of our Hussars as came from Germany.

When the mountains were passed, we found ourselves in Andalusia. A sensible difference was then experienced in the warmth of the atmosphere; and the grandeur of the prospect which expanded before us, formed a striking contrast to the barren black mountains we had just crossed. The farmers were busy with the olive harvest, and the landscape presented that cheerful animated aspect about the close of winter, which is only witnessed in more northern countries during the harvest or vintage months.

On our left were the mountains of the kingdom of Jaen; and in the distance we could see the summits of the Sierra-Nevada of Grenada, permanently covered with snow. These heights were the last retreats of the Moors before they were finally expelled from Spain.

The road lay through extensive olive-plantations, under whose protecting shade grew alternately the corn and the vine. The fields were bordered with hedges of aloes, whose leaves were as sharp as lances, and whose tapered stems shot upwards to the height of trees. Here and there, behind the habitations, we perceived thick planted orange-orchards, and on the unploughed borders of the streams grew laurels of a lively whiteness, which were then in flower. A few old palm-trees were still seen at intervals, which the clergy preserved in their gardens, that they might have their branches to distribute on Palm Sundays.

We marched either on the one or the other side of the Guadalquiver, and followed the windings of the river in its course between Andujar and Cordova. The country becomes less picturesque in approaching Seville. Sometimes we crossed fields of corn several miles in length, without meeting with a tree or a house, and at other times we passed over uncultivated tracts, where we saw only flocks of sheep.

Andalusia is, without doubt, the most fertile and the naturally richest country of Spain. It is a common proverb in La Mancha and the Castiles, that "the very water of the Guadalquiver, fattens more horses than the barley of other countries." The bread of Andalusia is reckoned the whitest and sweetest in the world, and the olives there are of a prodigious size. The climate is so pure and mild, that one may sleep almost the whole year in the open air. During the summer, and sometimes even in winter, people are seen sleeping all night under open porticos. A number of individuals not burdened with riches, travel without ever concerning themselves to seek shelter for the night. They carry their own provision, or purchase such food as women prepare for passengers, on chaffing dishes, at the entrance, or on the public squares, of great cities. The poor never ask each other, as is the case farther north, if they have a house to inhabit, but if they have a good cloak to keep out the suns heat, or to screen them from the winter rains.

At every step in Andalusia, more so than anywhere else in the Peninsula, the traveller meets with remains and memorials of the ancient Arabs. It is the singular blending together of Eastern manners and customs with Christian usages, that chiefly distinguishes the Spanish people from all other Europeans.

The houses, in towns, are almost all constructed in the Moorish fashion. Within, they have a paved court of large flagstones, in the middle of which there is a basin, where fountains perpetually spout their waters, and refrigerate the air, under the shade of citron or cyprus-trees. Trellis-work of oranges is sometimes supported on the walls; and these trees carry all the year round their leaves, fruits, and flowers. The different apartments communicate with each other through the court. There is generally a porch within the gate, which opens to the street. In the ancient palaces of the Moorish kings and nobles—as, for instance, in the Alhambra of Grenada—these courts have peristyles or porticos running round them, whose numerous narrow arches are supported by very tall and elegant columns. Common houses have but a very plain small inner court, with a cistern in one corner, shaded by a lofty citron-tree. A kind of pitcher or jar, in which water is put to cool, is generally suspended near the door of such houses, or where there is a current of air. These pitchers are called *alcarazas*, an Arabic word, which shows that they were introduced into Spain by the Moors. The Cathedral of Cordova, which is an ancient mosque, has within its walls one of these open courts. Like private houses, this court is shaded by citrons and cypresses, and contains basins constantly supplied with the living stream by upright jets of water. On entering the consecrated part of the mosque, or *mezquita*, for its ancient name is still retained, the sight of so many marble columns of different colours strikes the beholder with astonishment. These columns stand in parallel rows pretty near each other, and support a kind of open arcade, covered above with wood. These numerous columns, with arcades overhead, are like a vast forest of palms, whose branches are regularly trained, and unite together, as they hang downwards.

The chapel where the book of the law was kept, is now; however, sacred to St Peter. In the middle of that ancient Mohammedan mosque, but now Christian temple, is placed the great altar for mass, and a choir where the canons chant the service of God. These transmutations are frequently to be met with in Spain, and mark the triumph of Christianity over Islamism.

The Andalusians rear immense flocks, which are fed on the plains in winter, and are driven to the mountains to seek their food about their tops during summer. The practice of transmigrating with their flocks to such. an extent at certain seasons every year, is derived from Arabia, where is is of great antiquity.

The Andalusian horses are descended from the generous breed which the Arabians brought with them long ago; and the same distinctions of pure and noble extraction, common among them, still exist in Spain. The horse of Andalusia is a spirited, lively, and gentle animal. The sound of the trumpet delights and inspires him; the noise and smoke of the powder do not affright him. He is most sensible of his masters words and caresses, who never strikes, but flatters and encourages him when oppressed with fatigue. The horse seems then to gather new strength, and sometimes does, from emulation and a wish to please, what no blows could have compelled him to perform.

We had frequently some Spanish peasants attending us, conveying our baggage, provisions and ammunition, on their horses and mules. I once heard one of these peasants, after a long address to his horse, which was quite exhausted, whisper eagerly with a low voice in the ear of the animal, as if to spare him a general disgrace—"Take care lest you be seen." A boy just at the time was beating his ass with all his strength, and cursing the mother that began her. The asses are not treated so gently as the horses are, being reckoned quite insensible to honour.

A journey in Spain is commonly made on horseback, and goods are transported in some of the provinces on the backs of mules. The excellent roads which traverse Spain, are quite of modern origin. The streets of ancient towns are narrow and crooked, and each story of the houses projects the farther outwards, the higher it ascends. It is evident that such streets, which are of Moorish origin, were never made for carriages. The Andalusian and Spanish inns, excepting some in great cities built by Italians, are just large caravansaries, where the traveller gets only a lodging for himself and for his horses and mules. He must carry his own provisions with him, and sleep on his horse-cloth. The natives of the country travel in companies, when they leave the frequented roads. They carry fire-arms suspended at their saddle-bows, for fear of being robbed by the smugglers that infest the mountains of Grenada, and those of the south coast between Malaga and Cadiz. The country people, and particularly farm-servants, in some parts of Spain and Andalusia, are accustomed to sleep on mats, which they roll up and often carry about with them. This Eastern custom is a comment on our Saviours command to the paralytic person in scripture. "Take up thy bed, and walk."

The custom of sitting *à la Mauresque*, on round mats made of rushes, is still observed by women of the lower orders. In some convents of Spain also, where ancient manners are transmitted without change, the nuns still delight to sit like the Turks, without knowing that they are imitating the enemies of the Christian faith. A kind of veil of woollen stuff, called a mantilla, commonly worn by females in Andalusia, which conceals sometimes the whole face except the eyes, seems to be copied from the fashion that the Eastern women have of wrapping themselves in large scarfs of the same manufacture when they go out of doors. The Spanish dances, particularly those of the fandango kind, very much resemble the wanton manner of the East. Their way of playing the castanets dancing, and singing *seguidillas*, still exist in Arabia and Egypt, as well as in the Peninsula. A scorching wind which blows from the east is still called in Andalusia the Medina wind.

The Andalusians and Spaniards in general, are religiously sober, like the Orientals, even in the midst of plenty. They regard intemperance as the abuse of Gods gifts, and despise those who are its slaves. Salt pork is daily eaten at their meals. This unwholesome article of food in hot climates, is forbidden by the sacred law of every Eastern nation, and they heartily detest it. When the Christians reconquered Spain, and before the Moors were completely expelled, there were many Mussulmans and Jews in Andalusia, who, for permission to stay still, assumed an aspect of conversion. The Spanish Christians then ate pork, in order to be known as such; and this test was, so to speak, a "profession of their faith."

There is such a striking analogy, even now, between the mode of fighting in some parts of Spain, and that of the different hordes of Arabians with whom the French fought on the banks of the Nile, that if one was to substitute Spanish, in place of Arabic names, on some pages of the history of the Egyptian campaign, it might pass for an account of the Spanish war.

The levies *en masse* of Spanish national and local troops fight in disorder, and charge with horrid cries. In an attack on level ground, they are distinguished, like the Arabians, by their impetuosity and their fury, mingled with despair and fanaticism. Like that race also, they often too soon abandon the prospect of success, and give up the contest even at the moment when they might claim the victory; but when they fight behind walls or intrenchments, they stand to the last. The inhabitants of Egypt fled beyond the desert to the fastnesses of their mountains. The people of Spain abandoned their homes at the approach of our troops, and carried their most precious effects to the hills. In Spain as in Egypt, our soldiers dared not loiter a step behind the army, at the peril of their lives. In fine, the people of South Spain cherish in their souls the same spirit of deep and lasting hatred, and yet the same lively fancy, which characterize the people of the East. Like them. they are discouraged by the least rumour of defeat, ansi rise in arms continually at the most distant prospect of success. The Spaniards, like the Arabians, often manifest the most horrid excess of cruelty to their prisoners, and at other times treat them with the noblest and most generous hospitality.

After passing Andujar, Cordova, Essica, and Carmona, we arrived at Seville, where we received orders from Marshal Soult to rejoin our regiment at Ronda, a town distant about ten leagues from Gibraltar. At first, we were struck at the deep tranquillity which reigned throughout Andalusia, most of the principal cities having sent deputations to King Joseph. But this peace was only apparent, and existed only in the plains where we had numerous troops. The inhabitants of the kingdoms of Murcia, Grenada, and those of the province of Ronda—those, in a word, that dwell among the mountains which cross, surround, and border on Andalusia, or divide it from Estremadura and Portugal—all these had simultaneously taken arms.

We left Seville on the 18th of March, and slept at Outrera. On the 19th, we passed on to Moron, a small town at the foot of the Ronda mountains. The inhabitants of that place were on the eve of joining the mountaineers, who had been in arms for some time. The greater part of the population of Moron assembled in the great square on our arrival. The men regarded us with an expression of restrained fury, and seemed to watch our minutest movements. It was not to gratify a harmless curiosity, but to inure their eyes to the sight of enemies whom they intended soon to attack, and thus to dispel that fear of the future which acts so powerfully on imaginative people. Some females were dressed in cloth of English manufacture, on which were depicted the portrait of King Ferdinand VII, and those of the Spanish generals most distinguished in battle with the French.

When we witnessed the incitement and spirit of revolt which reigned throughout the town, we resolved on lodging all together in three adjoining inns. If we had separated to seek accommodation in the houses up and down, as we might have done with safety in the plain, we would doubtless have all been dead next morning.

We had but a very few men capable of combat, having many spare horses to lead, and the military chest, and equipments for the regiment conveyed by requisition. asses and mules, to attend to besides, which greatly retarded and impeded our march. A quarter-master and I were the only individuals in the detachment that had before been in Spain, or could speak the language. The former kept always beside the adjutant-major in command, to act as his interpreter. I rode always an hours journey a-head of the troops, to secure provisions and lodgings in places where we meant to rest.

Leaving Moron, we entered the mountains of Ronda, on our way to Olbera. I passed on as usual in advance of the troop to secure our quarters, and was accompanied by a Hussar, and a young brigadier-chef to act as a scout, chosen from the recruits for the occasion. About two leagues from Moron, I knocked at the door of a farmhouse among the mountains, and was answered by an elderly man in much agitation. I asked for something to drink, which he instantly supplied with extraordinary zeal. I learned afterwards, that a band of five armed smugglers were stationed in the house, and were alarmed lest they might be discovered.

The advanced guard soon after making its appearance, I was afraid I would not have time to prepare lodgings and provisions before the detach. meat arrived. We could only move at a slow pace, from the steep and rugged nature of the road, and because our horses were jaded with a march of several months. I gave my horse in charge to the Hussar, and mounted that of the guide we had taken at Moron. I went on before my companions, and arrived in sight of Olbera unattended.

A deep valley denuded of trees, into which the road suddenly descends, lay between me and the town, built on a steep rocky eminence which commands the whole country. The peasants at work in the neighbouring fields united in bands of eight or ten as I advanced, and, according to custom, inquired among themselves, with concern, what could be the cause of my arrival. They then left their labours, and followed in the path behind me. The towns people had observed me for some time, and were out in crowds on the rocks to get a better view.

I began to fear that there were no French in Olbera, as I had believed; and therefore halted at the bottom of the valley, surprised at the in-creasing agitation which I perceived. I hesitated for a moment if I should not return, but I thought it my duty to press on at every peril. My horse was already much fatigued with its journey, and I must have returned by a road exceedingly steep. Besides, I was followed at no distance by a troop of labourers, armed with mattocks. These people soon came up and surrounded me, inquiring from what province I was, where I was going, and what news I brought. I saw at once, from these questions, that they imagined I was in the Spanish service—my uniform being of a deep brown colour had caused this error.

I took care not to correct them, not knowing if I dared do it without danger to my life. I hoped to gain time until my detachment would arrive, and gave them to understand that I was a Swiss officer in the service of the Junta; that I was going to Gibraltar; and added, to put them in good humour, that the Marquis de la Romana had just gained a great victory near Badajos. The peasants received these news with eagerness, and narrated them over again to each other, cursing the French with a thousand imprecations, which gave me a dismal idea of the fate awaiting me, if I should happen to be known.

I asked, in my turn, if there were any of these detested Frenchmen in their village? They replied, that King Joseph had been beaten at Gaucin with all his guards, that he had evacuated Ronda some days ago, and that, by this time, that city must have been occupied by 10,000 guerillas. It was at Ronda we had orders to join our regiment; and if it was indeed in other hands, our detachment had no other fate to expect among the mountains but inevitable destruction.

The peasants turned aside to quench their thirst at a spring, and I continued to climb the hill by myself. Soon after I perceived five men, armed and equipped like soldiers, who hastened by another path to get before me, and entered Olbera before I arrived. From the noise I heard immediately after, I conceived they must have brought~the news of the advance of my troop, and that I was discovered. I again stopped, doubting if I should proceed.

The inhabitants, observing me from the rocks, saw my uncertainty, and redoubled their shouts. The women, in great numbers, had posted themselves on a hill which commanded the entrance of the village; and their shrill voices, mingling with those of the men, fell on the ear like a tempest of whistling winds. I formed the resolution to ad vance. It would have been certain death to return. It would have been an acknowledgment of guilt, which rarely finds mercy from an irritated mob.

I was then met by a *corregidor*, an *Alcaid* and two priests, preceded by five or six persons, with a young man at their head, whom I afterwards found out to be the *Gracioso* of the place. With a deriding manner, he said to me in Spanish:

"You will be well received by the ladies of Olbera; they are truly fond of the French;" and many other such sneering speeches.

One of his companions demanded in a stern voice, "What number of French were behind?"

I replied, "About two hundred, more or less."

"It is false," said he, with sufficient rudeness; "there is not a hundred, including yourself; these five men that have just come in, saw them at the farmhouse on the road from Moron."

I now had reason to believe they knew who I was. The *corregidor* and the priests approaching, I thought for an instant, from their ungracious aspect, that they were about to propose I should receive extreme unction. Amid the uproar, I could plainly hear these words:

"Hang him, he is a Frenchman! He is the devil himself! He is an incarnate devil!"

In a minute, to my great surprise, I saw the Spaniards disperse. The brigadier-chef, the Hussar, and the guide I had left behind, happened just then to appear on the opposite heights. Those who were stationed on the most elevated of the rocks, took them for the vanguard of my detachment; and, by shouts and signs, signified their approach to the multitude around me.

The *corregidor* and *Alcaid* soon assumed a different manner. They told me, quite humbly, that they were the magistrates of the place, and that they paid their respects to me in obedience to the mandate of King Joseph, which ordained, that the constituted authorities throughout Spain should go out to meet the French, and treat them with attention. My confidence increasing with their submission and fears, I advised them, with some threats, to keep the multitude under authority; and ordered them instantly to prepare provisions for the troop.

The *corregidor*, by way of excusing their conduct, prayed that no notice might be taken of the behaviour of a few drunken fellows, who took delight in exciting the mob. When I inquired who the five armed men were, I had seen entering the village some minutes before, one of the clergymen replied, with an affected tone, and rather ironically, that they had been a bird-shooting, and that the bags they bore were filled with game. With this very lame excuse I was obliged to be contented. I alighted and walked on foot, with the priests and *Alcaid*, to the guildhall in the great square at the head of the town, and commenced writing the soldiers billets along with them.

The brigadier-chef who followed, having left the Hussar with my horse at the entrance of the town, arrived at the gallop soon after, before the door of the house where I was. He had scarcely touched the ground, when the Spaniards rushed into the streets around, with shouts of savage fury. They expected to see a powerful troop, but when only one man rode through their village, they recovered from their mistake, and left their houses in a rage. So great was their vehemence, that they crushed each other in an arched way, which leads to the public square. Instantly I went to the balcony, and called on the brigadier-chef, who, having come up, we shut ourselves in the council-room, and barricaded the door. The crowd halted for a moment to seize the brigadier-chef's horse, pistols, and portmanteau. The leaders of the tumult then took possession of the staircase, and ascended to the door of the apartment in which we had enclosed ourselves, with the *corregidor* and the priests; and they called out to us through the partition instantly to surrender.

At. first I endeavoured, by means of the *corregidor*, whom I held fast, to order them to remain quiet, and told them our detachment would very soon arrive. I declared our determination to sell our lives dearly, and, if they dared to enter, their father priest would fall the first victim to their fury. Believing the door would be broken open, I retired some steps to the narrow entrance of the inner chamber, and kept hold of the parson as a shield to defend me in extremity. I drew my sabre, ordered the brigadier-chef to do the same, and to remain at the end of the room to prevent the curate and the *corregidor* from taking hold of me.

The shouts of the people grew louder and louder; and the inhabitants who came to speak with us, were driven back by those who had seized the staircase and the square. The door was violently shaken, end began to give way to the united efforts of the mob. I then said to the parson—"Forgive me, Father you see I cannot restrain the populace; I am compelled by necessity to make you share my fate, and we must die together."

The curate, terrified at the danger which threatened his brother as well as himself, advanced to the balcony, and called aloud to the inhabitants, that their priest would perish for a certainty, if they did not instantly retire. The women, hearing these words, uttered a yell of agony, and the crowd, with one sudden unanimous movement, fell back. The veneration of these people for their priests is most sincere and profound.

For some time longer the brigadier-chef and I sustained this deadlock. Soon after the place became quiet, and the shouts of the enraged rabble were hushed. The trampling of horses feet belonging to my detachment, which was forming in line at the lower end of the village, was now beard. The sound reached us all of a sudden, as distinctly as if it had been the deep hour of midnight.

In company with the *corregidor* and the parson, we now rejoined our troop. We took the clergyman with us as a safeguard. I related to my comrades the history of my reception, and advised them to proceed to Ronda the same day, after the horses were fed. In spite of all my remonstrances, the adjutant-major in command insisted on sleeping at Olbera, telling me, with a kind of reproach, "that it was a thing unknown for regular troops to discommode themselves for a few peasants." This officer had just come from France, where he had spent several years in the depot of his regiment, and knew nothing of the Spaniards.

We bivouacked in a meadow around the walls, near

to an inn on the road below the village. The inhabitants were apparently quite peaceful during the remainder of the day, and supplied us with provisions. But in place of a young ox, which I had ordered, they brought us an ass cut into quarters. The Hussars discovered that the veal, as they called it, had a very insipid taste. It was not long till we learned, from their own mouths, the strange deception these people had practised on us. They often cried to us afterwards while they fired, "You fed on asses flesh at Olbera." The most deadly insult that can be offered to a Christian, they think, is to make him eat ass-flesh.

Not. having courage to attack us in our enclosure, they prepared to do it as we departed. They sent word to the inhabitants of the neighbouring villages, to place ambuscades, and to lie in wait for us, on our way next day to Ronda. Toward the evening they assumed a threatening aspect. They went to the rocks in great numbers, and formed a thick barrier around the access to our bivouack. Thus they remained, quite immoveable, surveying our slightest motions. Now and then some voices insulting the sentries broke on the stillness of the hour, but were instantly suppressed by the *Alcaids*.

When it was pretty late, the parson presented himself before our bivouack, and begged to speak with me. He said that he had provided excellent lodgings for our officers, and pressed me earnestly to induce my comrades to accept them. His intention was, as we have since learned, to make us all prisoners; hoping that the soldiers, finding themselves without officers would, next morning, become coinfused as to their next course of action.

I hesitated not to refuse his offer. The priest then inquired if I cherished any resentment for what had passed in the forenoon, and if I had any suspicion of the designs of the inhabitants. I replied, that I had neither resentment nor mistrust. He then entreated me just to go home with him, saying it was his wish to treat me well. I consulted with my fellow-officers, and it was agreed that I should go unaccompanied to the village, to show the inhabitants that we had no design of vengeance, and thus discourage them from attacking us at night. My comrades hoped that I would be able to send them some supper too. I again returned to the priest, and asked his sacred word that I would sustain no harm. He immediately gave it; and to prove my implicit confidence, I gave my sword to the sentinel in his presence, and accompanied him unarmed.

We passed through the town together. On every side the inhabitants as we passed made low reverences to my guide, but regarded me with menace. When they came so near as to make me be afraid of attack, the priest, by a glance or a frown, compelled them to retire. Such was the deference paid him on account of his sacred calling.

We arrived at the house, and were received by his housekeeper. She was a tall woman, about thirty-five or forty years old. She first offered us chocolate and biscuits, and then served our supper at a table near the kitchen-fire. I sent off some supper to my comrades, and took my place at the table. The priest sat opposite, and his housekeeper sat down to his right, almost under the chimney, which was very elevated. After a moments silence, the priest inquired if I would not go to mass next morning before I left the place; I replied, that I was not a Catholic. At these words his countenance altered; and his housekeeper, who had never seen a heretic, startled in her chair, made some unconscious exclamations, and sighed deeply. After uttering several *Ave Marias* between her teeth, she looked at the priest, to judge how she ought to feel at the sight of such a terrible apparition as a heretic. (The popular descriptions, and the pictures in many country churches, represent heretics with darting flames from their mouths). The housekeeper resumed her composure, when she saw the priest carry on the conversation at his ease.

After supper, I was invited to sleep there, the priest declaring I must be much fatigued, and that he could give me a bed at least as good as our bivouack. Seeing I hesitated in my reply, he added, that it would be advisable to let the crowd disperse, and that I ought to wait a few hours. I then began to suspect that he intended to keep me in his house, and to deliver me to the populace. I was afterwards told this was in fact his design, and that he was the leader of the insurrection. Some reasons, however, have since induced me to believe, that, in detaining me a prisoner, he wished to save me from the doom determined by the inhabitants of the village and himself against my detachment.

As I was wholly in his power, I took care not to manifest the smallest symptom of distrust. I told him that I accepted his offers, in perfect confidence of my safety, since he had pledged his sacred word, and that I would go to sleep; but I begged he would awaken me in two hours at the latest, because my comrades, not seeing me return before midnight, would probably leave their bivouack, and set the town on fire. The priest showed me to the adjoining chamber. I went to bed—a luxury we seldom enjoyed in Spain; and he took away the lamp, after wishing me a good night.

The darkness of my situation did not now help to let me see the bright side of my fate. I repented having left my sabre. I regretted it as a faithful friend, that could have given me good counsel in my need. I listened, and heard the murmurs of people in the street, passing and repassing, under my windows. The priest from time to time gently opened the door, and put in his white head, with the lamp in his right hand, to see if I was asleep. I feigned a deep slumber, and he quietly retired.

Several men entered the next room. They talked at first in a low tone of voice, but afterwards, in confusion, and all together. Then, all at once they fell quiet, as if they feared they would awake me, or that I might be listening to their discourse. I spent two hours almost in this agitated awkward situation, ruminating what course I ought to pursue. I determined on calling the priest. He came immediately. I told him I wished instantly to join my troop. He laid down the lamp without saying a word, and left me, no doubt to consult with the Spaniards who were in the house, what he ought to do with me.

Who should enter my chamber at this moment, to my great joy, but our quartermaster, who spoke Spanish. He was accompanied by the *corregidor*. My comrades, he told me, were concerned about my fate; and had sent him to inquire what had befallen me. He said the inhabitants already considered me their prisoner; that they designed to attack us next day; and declared that not one of us would be suffered to escape.

I dressed with speed, and again reminded the priest of his sacred promise; telling him, my comrades threatened to take arms if I did not immediately return. Fortunately for me, the preparations for a general rising were not yet completed. The priest could no longer detain me. He called the *corregidor* and an *Alcaid*, with a few others, who placed us in the middle of their number, and led us through the crowd to our bivouack.

The quartermaster who was fortunately sent to me, was a Norman, of as good metal as the steel of his sword. Under the appearance of his good nature, he concealed all the cunning peculiar to his countrymen. He gained the confidence of the inhabitants, by telling them that he was the son of an officer of the Walloon guards, detained a prisoner in France with Charles IV—that he had been compelled to serve with us—and, for a long time, had sought an opportunity of deserting. The Spaniards of the mountains are, by turns, as cunning and as credulous as savages. They believed this story, sympathized with the wily Norman, gave him money, and intrusted him with part of their plans. Through him we gained knowledge of the intention of the neighbouring villages to make a united attack on us, in great numbers, at a dangerous defile on the road to Ronda. That knowledge saved us from a total defeat.

As we were going to depart next day, the priest and the *corregidor* came requesting a letter of witness to show to the French who might afterwards visit Olbera, that we had been treated with attention. They trusted that the threatening appearance of the populace would have made us do as they desired. We replied that it could not be granted, unless they delivered up the arms taken from the brigadier-chef's horse the preceding evening. We had several times before demanded them, but to no purpose.

The *corregidor* and the priest took the road in silence, leading to the top of the village; and very shortly after their departure, cries of alarm were heard. The inhabitants had just murdered six Hussars and two farriers, who imprudently went to shoe their horses at the smithy. Then the shooting commenced. We instantly took to horse; and the body of the detachment followed the adjutant-major who commanded us to the place of rendezvous, about a gun-shot from the town. I remained at the bivouac, and kept with me ten Hussars to guard the retreat and secure the baggage, with which the mules were not yet loaded, the drivers, who were Spaniards, having fled during the night.

One of my comrades, soon after, came to me to say, that our rear guard would be surrounded, and that the enemy kept up a constant fire against the troops from the rocks above and the windows at the end of the village through which we had to pass. Having no chance of assistance, we determined to take a route through the midst of our foes. My horse was shot through the neck, and fell. I speedily raised him, and reached the detachment. My comrade had his arm broken with a ball. One after another, I witnessed nearly all the Hussars fall who followed me. Women, or rather exasperated furies, threw themselves on the wounded with horrid screams, and vied with each other in putting them to death with the cruelest torments. They put knives and scissors in their eyes, and exulted with savage joy at the sight of their blood. The excess of just rage against the invaders of their country, seemed to have changed their nature to the very core.

Our detachment all this time had kept waiting for us, facing the enemy. The inhabitants dared not leave their rocks and their houses, nor could we get at them on horseback, to avenge the death of our companions. We called over our numbers in their sight, placed the wounded in the centre of the troop, and slowly again began our march.

Being unable to find a guide, and ignorant of the road, we took the first path which led away from the beaten track, on which we knew the mountaineers were lying in wait. We wandered about for some time at random. At length we saw a man riding on a mule, making haste to get away from a farmhouse. I followed and overtook him. Having placed him between two Hussars of the advanced guard, I commanded him to direct us to Ronda, or take his choice of being stabbed. Without this peasant, whom we happened on by chance, it would have been quite impossible for us to find the way in this unknown and hostile region.

This is an example of the difficulties we bad constantly to struggle with, not merely of a military nature, or such as might be foreseen and met with in the routine of regular war, but obstacles without number which Spanish resistance generated, and were encountered wherever we went.

After entering a pretty extensive valley, we perceived on the heights towards the left a troop of a thousand or fifteen hundred men observing our march. Among them we could distinguish some women and even children. They were the inhabitants of Settenil and the villages around, who, having learned that we had changed our road to avoid their ambuscade, had set off to pursue us. They were making all the haste possible, in hopes of getting between us and the passage of a defile in our front.

We trotted our horses to get there before them, and happily cleared the pass. Immediately after this, we were surrounded by a host of peasants, who separated tumultuously from the main body of the enemy, and kept firing on our flank. They followed us among the rocks, never venturing nearer than a gun-shot, lest they would be unable to regain the mountains if we made a charge. Priests and *Alcaids* rode on horseback over the heights and directed the movements of the crowd. Such of our Hussars as had the misfortune to be wounded and to fall, were in a moment mercilessly stabbed. One alone escaped. He had the presence of mind to say, that he wished to confess before he died, and the minister of Settenil saved him from their fury.

We reached a frequented path on the side of a steep mountain. Here we halted for some minutes to rest our horses. The rocks overhead screened us from the fire of the enemy above. At length we came in sight of Ronda. As we were rejoicing at the prospect of terminating our journey, we were struck at the sight of fresh enemies firing briskly from an ambush in a wood near the town. Our uneasiness now became extreme, for we feared that the French had abandoned the place. But with the most heartfelt joy, we beheld a party of Hussars belonging to our own regiment coming to meet us. At a distance they had mistaken us for enemies.

We entered the town, and halted in the public square. Our comrades now came to embrace us, and to hear the news from France and the rest of the world, to which they had become almost total strangers. We then dispersed into our different quarters, calculating on at least a few days rest, after the fatigues we had for so long endured.

Chapter 8

MOUNTAIN GUERILLAS

Ronda is situated among high mountains, which must be crossed in going to Gibraltar, and are generally known by the name of the Serrania de Ronda. Their summits are free of vegetation, and their sides are covered with a brittle rock, whose surface, one would think, the sun's heat for ages had blackened and calcined. It is only at the bottom of valleys, and on the borders of streams, that meadows and orchards are to be found. Nearer the sea, the vines creep along the ground almost without culture. From thence come the Spanish wines held in greatest repute.

Constantly obliged to struggle under the privations of uncivilized life, the people who live in these barren mountains are sober, tenacious and unconquerable. Religion is the only tie which binds them, and almost the only of controlling them. The late Spanish government could never subject them to a strict observance of the laws in time of peace, nor oblige them to serve in the armies during war. They uniformly ran off, when marched away from their habitations.

Each village chooses its *Alcaids* for a term of two years. These magistrates, however, seldom dare to exercise their authority, for fear of making themselves enemies, and of being exposed to an always implacable vengeance. If one of the king's judge had a mind to use force to quell a disturbance, in an instant every dagger would be turned against him. But if a prayer was commenced, those who threatened with daggers would lay aside their fury, to join in with one accord. In their hottest quarrels, the arrival of the holy sacrament never fails to restore peace.

I was informed, that no feast of any consequence ever occurs in the Sierra, without the death of two or three individuals. Jealousy and rivalry among these people takes place in a frenzy which blood alone can satiate. It seldom fails that the mortal stab follows the sidelong glance of passion.

These highlanders, to a man almost, are contraband traders. They sometimes unite in great numbers from different villages, under their most noted chiefs, and, descending into the plains, disperse themselves about the country to carry on their illegal traffic. Often they resist the troops sent in pursuit of them. These smugglers have always been celebrated for their cunning, and for the skilfulness with which they avoid hosts of watchful customs officers. Ranging through the mountains day and night, they are familiar with the most hidden caves, with all the passes, and with the least used paths.

Whilst the men are constantly engaged in their smuggling activities, the women remain in their mountainous villages, and engage in the most arduous work. They bear heavy loads with ease, and are proud of this superiority of strength, which they have gained by their toil. They have even been seen wrestling with each other, and contending who would lift the largest stones. When they go down to Ronda, they are known at once by their masculine size, their robust limbs, their curiousity and their proud looks. They are fond of ornamenting themselves when they visit the city, with the veils and rich items of contraband. Their style of dress makes a strange contrast with their coarse features and dark sunburnt complexions.

The warlike inhabitants of these lofty mountains had all taken arms against the French. When King Joseph came to Ronda at the head of his guards, about three weeks before our arrival, he vainly endeavoured to make them submit to his authority, first by gentle means, and then by force.

King Joseph remained only a few days at Ronda. He had left a garrison in that city, consisting of 250 Hussars of our regiment, and 300 soldiers of his own guard of infantry. He had given our Colonel, when he departed, the title of "Civil and Military Governor", with almost unlimited power over the neighbouring provinces. The absolute authority attached to this title, which was equal to that of captain-general, should have extended over a track of country fifteen or twenty leagues in circumference. But the smugglers of the Sierra, limited our sway to the walls of Ronda, and even there we could not sleep without anxiety, on account of our mistrust of the inhabitants of the suburbs.

The same night that I arrived, a number of fires were lighted successively on the mountains around. The deception occasioned by the darkness, made the flame of the most distant appear near, and it was observed by someone, that a burning circle surrounded us. The enemy had taken up their position before the city, with the intention of attacking us next day.

For half an hour we heard the sound of a goats horn repeated again and again, which seemed to come from a grove of olives, beyond the old town, in a little valley below. We were passing a thousand jokes about these unmodulated notes, without being able to understand their meaning, when a Hussar from one of the advanced posts came at the gallop to tell the Colonel that a messenger from the enemy had come, demanding admission. The Colonel ordered him to be admitted, and the brigadier brought him immediately, after covering his eyes. The messenger told us, that he had come to propose we should surrender ourselves. He said, that the General of the mountain guerillas, with 15,000 men, had occupied every pass by which we could escape; that he had taken a French convoy carrying 50,000 cartridges, which were intended for us; and that he knew we could not defend the place for any length of time, because we had almost no ammunition. True it was, that the infantry of the garrison had but three rounds each. Our Hussars could make no use of the sabre among the rocks, where their horses proved of no advantage, and tended rather to hinder.

Our colonel replied to the messenger that we would first sit down to table. He gave me a sign to conduct our newcomer to the messroom, recommending him to my attention. He was a young man of a pretty good appearance—he wore a round hat after the Andalusian fashion, and a short brown vest trimmed with sky-blue chain-lace. His only mark of distinction was a scarf in the manner of the country, with a few silver threads unwoven at the ends. In place of a sabre, he wore a long, straight, old-fashioned sword.

At first he was embarassed to see himself, in his modest costume, among so many officers covered with embroidery. When we all put our hands to our sabres to unloose them before sitting down to eat, he showed some uneasiness, being unaware of the cause of this movement. I believe he thought we were going to kill him, in retaliation for a murder committed by the people of a neighbouring village some days before, on a public functionary of Ronda, whom we had sent to them as our messenger.

I soon dispelled his fears, by inviting him to unarm himself, and to take a seat along with us. After some moments silence, I asked him if he bad been long in the service of

Ferdinand VII? He replied, that he had only entered a year ago, as a lieutenant in the Cantabrian Hussars. Although enemies, I replied, we are doubly comrades, by the rank we hold, and the war in which we serve. He was much flattered by being reckoned an officer of regular troops. I put several questions to him about the leaders of the insurgent army. He vastly extolled the merits of General Gonzales, declaring him to be a man of uncommon talents in the art of war, and of a most profound knowledge in all military matters. We had never heard the name of that officer before; and it appeared afterwards that he was a sergeant of the line, whom the insurgents had dignified with the rank of Brigadier-General, that they might appear an organized force. By praising in exaggerated terms everything which concerned his own party, we came to know without his telling us, that no corps of English had left Gibraltar to join the mountain guerillas; which, had it been the case, would have rendered our situation perilous in the extreme.

The Spanish officer did not at first depart from that sobriety which characterizes his countrymen. But when we drank his health, he returned the compliment, and, following our example, he now attempted to keep up with us. We were only comrades at supper, but we were brothers at the dessert. We vowed an everlasting friendship; and, among other proofs of esteem, we promised to fight each other in single combat the very first time we should again meet.

After supper, the Colonel sent the Spanish messenger home without making any reply. I was directed to conduct him to the advanced posts of the enemy. I told him to tie up his eyes himself; and a Hussar, at his right hand, led his horse. I was on his left, and we took the road together towards Gibraltar, by which he had come. On passing the main-guard, we were joined by the messenger's trumpeter, and an old royal carabineer, who acted as his attendant. He was the only one the insurgent army could boast of; and was sent on this occasion, on account of a new uniform he wore, to do honour to their commissioner. I was astonished to hear him ask his officer, with a tone of authority, "Why have you made me wait so long?"

The trumpeter was a young shepherd, dressed in a green mantle, which formed a singular contrast with his sandals, his bonnet, and the rest of his rustic garments. He had got his lesson before he came away. When our Hussars inquired what had become of his trumpet, he said he happened to lose it. He had in fact purposely dropped the humble goats horn, which he had blown, fearing that the sight of that unwarlike instrument would destroy the illusion, which he hoped would be produced by his disguise. The shepherd could not get his horse to keep ahead of us. It stood, and kicked at every step. I called out to him in Spanish to "move on." He replied, most pitifully, "It is the first time ever I rode horse, and they have given me a worthless beast that will not stir an inch." The carabineer, who followed a few yards behind us, went up to the poor fellow, ordered him rudely to be silent, and ended his perplexity, by taking his horse by the bridle.

When we reached the first Spanish post, after passing the suburbs of the ancient town, I bade the deputy adieu, and returned to my colonel to give an account of what occured. A council of war being held, we came to the resolution of abandoning the city, and going to Campillos, to wait there for ammunition. This town is about seven leagues distant from Ronda, and is situated in a plain at the foot of the mountains, where our cavalry would give us an advantage over the highlanders, whatever might be their numbers. We put very little trust in the 300 men of King Joseph's guard, this corps being chiefly composed of Spanish deserters.

The Colonel ordered that the garrison should commense their march in half an hour, without a drum being beat or a trumpet blown, lest the enemy should be thereby advertised of our departure. I instantly summoned the quartermasters who were under my command, and we went from house to house to call up the recruits I had brought. They had calculated on making a long stay at Ronda to recover from the fatigues of their journey. When we went at midnight to warn them of our departure, they were in a profound sleep, and, not hearing the trumpet sound as usual, they were unwilling to believe our words. Some even thought we were the ghosts of their lieutenant and corporals, come to torment them in their dreams with orders to march. We were obliged to give them some hearty strokes, to prove our identity.

For two hours we marched in a profound silence, by the brilliant light of the olive wood fires, which the mountaineers had lighted on the tops of the hills in our vicinity. At daybreak, we halted for a quarter of an hour, in a small plain, where we could have used our sabres, to see if the enemy would venture an engagement. But they fled at our approach, and regained the summits of their mountains, without engaging. The peasants of the villages, on our march, fired at us from a distance. The women stationed themselves on the rocks above, to see us pass, and to rejoice at our retreat. They sung patriotic songs, in which they prayed for death to every Frenchman, to the Grand Duke de Berg, and to Napoleon. The burden of their verses was the imitation of a cock crowing, which is reckoned emblematical of France.

At length we reached Campillos, and saw perfectly well, by the manner of our reception, that the news of our losses at Olbera, and our retreat from Ronda had already reached this place. When I entered my lodging, I was very ungraciously welcomed by my landlord. My attendant having asked for a chamber near me, was shown into a dark, damp hole, which looked into a back yard. There having been no rations distributed when we arrived, the *Alcaid* had issued an order, enjoining the inhabitants to entertain the soldiers who were billeted on them. The Hussar who waited on me, made signs to the master of the house that he wanted some victuals. With a scornful air, I saw this person bring a small paltry table, on which there was a little bread and a few garlic cloves. I heard him say to his wife, "It is good enough for these French dogs; there is no need of being on ceremony with them now; they have been beaten, they are fleeing, and, please God and the Holy Mother, not one of them shall be in life two days hence." I pretended not to hear his execrations, that I might not let him know I understood his language.

I went out, and returned about an hour afterwards to my lodging, where I found a circle of five individuals sitting smoking cigars. They were in the habit of assembling every evening, as I understood, at the house of my host, who was a tobacconist. My Hussar sat at some distance, and on my entrance he rose and presented me his chair. I accepted it, and drew nearer to the fire. The Spaniards at first were silent; but one of them, to prove whether or not I understood Spanish, inquired if I was not very much fatigued. Though I seemed not to comprehend his meaning, he added, with a sneer, "You have made good use of your spurs for two days past?" I made no answer; and they concluded that I did not know a word of their language, and resumed their conversation.

They extolled, with boundless enthusiasm, the brave mountain men who had driven us out of Ronda. They related all the particulars of a most bloody battle that never happened, which lasted for twelve hours in the very streets of the city the evening before. They said our loss must have amounted to 600 men at least, and we had no more than 550 in all. They affirmed that the general of the mountaineers would attack us, within two days, that the inhabitants of the village would take up arms, and that they would annihilate these damned heretics, who were far worse than the Moors; "because," as they said, "these French neither believe in God, nor the Virgin, nor Saint Anthony, and not even in Saint James of Galicia. They do not even think it a crime to lodge in churches, and their horses with them." They repeated a thousand other such invectives, and excited their imaginations higher and higher. They concluded by saying, that "One Spaniard was a match for three Frenchmen;" and One of them added, that "he would kill half a dozen with his own hand."

I then rose and twice repeated the Spanish words *poco a poco*, which means "softly, softly." They seemed petrified to find that I had understood their whole conversation. I left them to tell my Colonel what I had just learned. he instantly commanded the *Alcaid* to disarm the village. The inhabitants delivered up their useless arms, but, as is usual in such cases, they retained those that were of any service.

On returning to my quarters, I found not one of my politicians. They had all taken flight. My host also had concealed himself. In my absence, his alarmed spouse had endeavoured to propitiate my Hussar. She had given him only water at first to quench his thirst, but now she brought him excellent wine. Having no idea that all this attention was the offspring of fear, and being much surprised at this unexpected kindness, he began to feel a certain impulse of vanity; and I found him, on my return, brushing up his horrible mustaches with more than ordinary complacency.

The moment I laid down my sabre, my hostess took it up, and carried it with great eagerness to the best apartment in the house, as if to take possession in my name. She then came trembling to entreat me not to cherish any resentment against her husband, telling me, that though he had not received me very politely at first, he was, however, an honest man, and had an excellent heart. I told her that her husband might return when he pleased, for I would not do him any injury if he would give me immediate notice of all that he could learn concerning the plans of the enemy or the inhabitants. I added, however, merely to frighten him, that if he failed to do it, I would have him hanged; and then I went to bed.

I rose at daybreak next morning, and, on opening my chamber-door, found my landlord waiting to appease me. Before saying a word, he presented me with a cup of chocolate and biscuits; which I accepted with great civility, and told him, that in future I would regulate my conduct towards him according to the vway in which behaved. He replied with a low bow, that I might do with him and his as I pleased.

We learned today, the 15th of March, that the Serranos had entered Ronda about an hour after our evacuation of it, and that they were preparing to attack us at Campillos. On the 16th, our colonel sent a strong detachment of a hundred Hussars and forty infantry to reconnoitre the enemy. I accompanied this expedition. We began our march at two hours before sunrise, and met the mountaineers about four leagues from Campillos. They had bivouacked all night on the side of a mountain, near the village of Caneta la Real. We halted about two gun-shots from them to examine their numbers and position. They were estimated to be about 4,000. When our observations were finished, we purposefully turned back along the road by which we had come.

The Serranos, seeing us preparing to return, believed

that we were afraid of them. They uttered loud cries, descended the mountain in a body, and, without observing any order, followed us for an hour in a very rugged and irregular tract of country. The ground becoming favourable for cavalry, they ended their pursuit and stopped to unite among the hills, and dared not at first advance into the plain. They then sent down some peasants to fire at the skirmishers of our rear guard, who had wheeled about, whilst the infantry and main body of the troop were crossing a wooden bridge over a torrent, which runs at the foot of a barren mountain, on whose summit the village of Teba is perched like an eagles erie.

The women of the village, clothed, according to the fashion of the country, in red and light blue dresses, were sitting on their heels in great numbers, on the top of the rocks, to witness the engagement, which they expected would immediately ensue. Our rear guard soon called in the sharpshooters, and began to pass the bridge. Then the women rose as one and sung a hymn to the Holy Virgin. At this signal the firing commenced; and the Spaniards, screened by the hill, poured down a shower of bullets all around us. We continued to pass the bridge under this discharge of musketry, without returning their fire. The women were observed to run down the rocks—to snatch the guns out of the hands of their husbands—and to place themselves in front, to oblige their men to advance and pursue us beyond the bridge.

Our rear guard, finding themselves rather closely pressed, faced the enemy; and the Hussars of the first line opened a well-directed fire from their carbines against the foremost of their number. Two were killed; the Spanish held back, and the women made all haste to reach the top of the mountain. However, about a hundred of the insurgents followed us at a distance, to within half a league of Campillos.

Next day a reconnoitring party of fifty Hussars found the Serranos encamped on the farther side of the wooden bridge, below the village of Teba. They went close up to them, and again returned at the same pace, without firing a single shot. The mountain men took courage, as they did the day before, and followed our scouts as far as our advanced posts. Our plan was to entice them into the plain before Campillos, and there to exercise our swords. The insurgents, being armed for the most part with fowling-guns, always had an advantage among the mountains, where the rocks hampered our pursuit of them. But in the plain they could not resist the charge of our cavalry, though much inferior in numbers, because of their indisciplined way of fighting.

At 10 a.m., I saw my host enter in a great hurry. He had a smile on his lips; but he rubbed his eyes, and vainly attempted to shed tears. He told me that we were all dead men; that our guards had been routed; and that 1,500 fierce guerillas were coming down to surround us in the plain, whilst the insurgent villagers attacked us in the streets. He clasped me warmly in his arms as if he pitied my approaching fate.

In fact, I heard that very moment the report of muskets, tumultuous shouts, and the noise of the trumpets and drums. People from all quarters were hastening to take arms. One of our picquets, stationed at no distance from the house where I lodged, had just been forced to retreat into the village. I soon mounted my horse and assembled my detachment. At the same instant the Colonel appeared, and ordered me to go to the aid of the guards who had been beaten. We made a sweeping charge in the plain—and it succeeded. Forty of our Hussars cut to pieces one hundred mountain men. Those left alive fled in the greatest fear. We returned when all was over, and the plain which had before resounded with the shouts of a host of musketeers, lay silent and strewn with the bodies of our slaughtered foes.

While we were thus engaged, the inhabitants of Camp-illos, thinking we would never return, put to death in their streets all those of our soldiers who had delayed going to the place of rendezvous, as they ought to have done, in case of an alarm. Our Hussars, on returning to the village, put to the sword every villager found with weapons, and it was with difficulty they could be restrained from pillage. The mountain guerillas dared no more show themselves in the plains. They marched the rest of the day, and part of the night, till they regained the high mountains in the vicinity of Ronda.

General Peremont came from Malaga to join us at Campillos on the 19th of March with three battalions of infantry, one regiment of Polish Lancers, and two can-nons. We received the ammunition we were in want of; and at six o'clock in the morning of the 20th, we all set off together to retake Ronda. We diverged a little from our route in passing Teba, to levy a contribution from its inhabitants, as a punishment for having taken arms three days before, even though they had made submissions to King Joseph.

Our Colonel left his regiment at the foot of the moun-tain, and ascended to the summit where the village is built, with only fifty Hussars. The inhabitants, being aware of our approach, and of the fine we had come to exact, had fled among the rocks with their most precious effects. Various articles abandoned on the road, indicated the track of their flight. The Colonel gave orders to break open the doors of some of the houses in the market-place, to see if any persons were concealed therein. They found only one poor old man, who, far from being afraid of the soldiers, uttered cries of joy when they came to him. They wished to profit by this expression of friendship, and to bring him from his hiding-place that they might get the information they wanted. But they soon observed that he was an idiot; and this was probably why his family or friends had left him behind.

We passed nearly two hours in the village, without finding a single individual that we could send to the scattered villagers, in order to relieve their fears, to say that nothing would be done to them, and that their offence would be forgiven, if they paid a contribution to King Joseph. We did not wish to make them irreconcilable enemies, and to drive them to despair by a rigorous revenge; though it was our duty not to allow their revolt to pass unpunished.

We devised the following plan to draw them from their hiding places. The Hussars burned some wet straw in the chimneys of some of the houses. These fires caused a dense smoke, which the wind blew among the mountains, and made the people believe their village was in flames. They hastened to send a deputation; and the *Alcaid* soon appeared, followed by four of the wealthiest citizens. He was dressed in a scarlet mantle and laced cap. No doubt he had attired himself in all his tokens of dignity; because he thought, in going to the French, he was rendering up his life as a sacrifice for the preservation of his village. The *Alcaid* promised that the contribution would be paid. We took him with us as a hostage, and he returned home in two days.

We halted for the night at a small village about four leagues distant from Campillos. We set out for Ronda on the 21st, at sunrise, and entered it without resistance. The mountain guerillas quickly abandoned the town on our approach, throwing down their muskets and cloaks in the streets, that they might more easily reach the mountains by the footpaths. The Hussars of our vanguard killed those who were slow to leave.

Some of the inhabitants of Ronda received us as liberators. The mountain men bad erected a gibbet in the

140

great square during our absence, in order to punish those of the citizens who had shown any favour to the French. If we had come a day later, many individuals would have been hanged. Thus private animosities would have been satisfied, under pretence of public vengeance. A magistrate was to have suffered, because he spurned a bribe in a smuggling affair some years before. A poor tailor, the night before we came, was thrown headlong from the rocks and dashed to pieces, because he had acted as an interpreter to our soldiers.

At daybreak of the same day when we had left Ronda the guerillas had entered it, with loud shouts and the firing of guns, as a manifestation of their joy. All the inhabitants of each village marched together tumultuously. Their women followed them, who were only distinguished from the men, as already described, by their clothing, their loftier stature, and a little more barbarity of manner.

They pretended that their husbands had reconquered Ronda from the French, and that everything in the town was theirs. Stopping before splendid mansions, they would say in their vanity to each other—"I make choice of this house; I shall be the lady of this one, and will come in a few days to stay in it, with my children and my goats." In the meantime, they loaded their asses with whatever they could find within the rooms. These ladies did not desist from plundering, till their poor animals were on the point of sinking under the weight of their burdens.

An English lieutenant, who went with them on the expedition, had his horse and portmanteau stolen, and could by no means get the guilty persons punished. The prisons were forced; and the offenders imprisoned therein ran, the moment they were at liberty, to wreak their vengeance on their judges and accusers. Debtors extorted from their creditors discharges for their debts. They committed to the flames all the chancery documents, that they might cancel every deed of mortgage held by any citizen upon their mountain properties.

The General-in-chief of the Serranos did not arrive at Ronda until six hours after we had left. He had endeavoured, first of all, to establish some kind of order in the town, with the assistance of what he called his regulars. Being unable to do so, he devised the following stratagem. He caused the public crier to announce that the French were returning. In the twinkling of an eye the guerillas assembled, and the inhabitants of the town had time to barricade their doors.

A person named Cura possessed the greatest influence over these indisciplined bands. He was a native of Valencia, where he had been a professor of mathematics. Having killed a man in a fit of jealousy, he took refuge among the illicit traders to escape from the pursuit of justice. He had secretly spread a report, that he was of noble birth, and that political reasons obliged him to remain unknown. The mountain people called him "The stranger with the big bonnet," because he wore a countryman's cap of a large size, in order to attract notice. That sort of mystery which hung about him, gave him great powers of persuasion over simpler folk. He extorted large contributions from several mountain villages about a month after, under the pretext of going to purchase arms and ammunition. He endeavoured to run off with the money intrusted to him, but was arrested and punished.

General Peremont had come to Ronda with his brigade, intent on making an expedition into the heart of the high mountains; but he was compelled to return to Malaga without making the attempt. He received intelligence that another body of insurgents had attacked that city in his absence. Ronda was again garrisoned by our

Hussars, and two hundred brave soldiers of Polish Infantry, in place of the battalion of King Joseph's guard we had with us previously.

The lofty platform on which Ronda stands, is of gentle ascent on every side but the north. It is separated on the south and west, from the mountains which command it, by a lovely cultivated valley. The Guadiaro river descends from the highest of these mountains, and divides the city. One might suppose, that the high rock on which it is built has been sundered by an earthquake, to form a deep crevice for the gloomy channel of this river.

The old city, on the left bank, is connected with the new town opposite, by a superb stone bridge with a single arch. Iron balconies project beyond the parapet walls on either side. The passenger is struck with a feeling of terror, when he sees unexpectedly below him, through the slender iron railings, at the depth of almost three hundred feet, the foaming river, like a single white thread, which the force of the torrent has impelled for ages through the awful abyss. A damp kind of fog constantly rises from the bottom of the gulf. The eye can scarcely distinguish; on account of the depth, the men and asses with their loads, who are always going up and down the winding path, to one of the mills constructed at the foot of the immense rocky terrace that supports the town.

In these times of war and trouble, we have sometimes witnessed, from the rocks above, the farmers of the valley leave their peaceful labours, to join the guerillas when they came rushing down to battle. From this spot also we have often seen the farmers bury their firearms in the ground, as our troops approached.

That part of Ronda which is called the old town, is almost entirely of Moorish origin. Its streets are narrow and crooked. The new town, on the other hand, is well built;

its squares are large, and its streets are wide and regular. By constructing some new works, and repairing an old castle, we easily put the old town into such a condition as to make it proof against a surprise attack; so that our infantry were quite able to defend it. Our Hussars were specially charged with the defence of the new town. We demolished some old walls, and levelled some uneven ground at the entrance to that part of the city; so that in case of danger, we might be able to repulse the enemy by charges of cavalry.

The guerillas encamped on the summits of the neighbouring heights, and night and day they watched all that took place in the city. When our trumpets sounded the reveillée, the shepherds horns were soon heard awakening our foes of the hills. They spent whole days harrying our picquets in one quarter or other, but took to flight the moment we went toward them, only to return later to trouble us further.

Whenever the Serranos were going to attack us, they commenced a loud shouting to animate them for the combat; and, long before their balls could reach us, they began to fire. The farthest off, hearing the cries and the shots, believed that their companions in front must have gained some superiority. Then they hurried on to take part in the action, that they might have their share of the honour of what they deemed an easy victory. With endless bravado, they passed those that once preceded them: and when they knew their error, it was impossible to retreat. We allowed them to come as far as the small plain around the new town, that we might attack them with the sabre; and they always withdrew after some of their number had been slain.

The most popular activity of the farm workers of Ronda, was to station themselves behind the rocks among the olives, at the end of the suburbs, and to smoke their cigars, and shoot our videttes. They would leave the town in the morning with their tools, as if they were going to work in the fields. There, or at the farmhouses, they would find their guns, and in the evening they would again return to Ronda unarmed, to sleep in the midst of us. It sometimes happened that our Hussars recognised their landlords among their antagonists. It was impossible to make a scrutiny sufficiently strict. If Marshal Soult's decree against the insurgent Spaniards had been executed, we would have been obliged to punish with death almost the whole population of the country. The French prisoners were hanged or burned alive by these people; they, on the other hand, when found armed, very seldom met with such punishments from our soldiers.

The Spanish women, the aged, and even the children, were all against us, and acted as spies. I saw a young boy, eight years old, come one day to play among our horses feet, and undertake to act as our guide. He led a small party of our Hussars into an ambuscade, and sheltered himself instantly among the rocks, tossing his cap into the air, and crying aloud, "Long live our King, Ferdinand VII!" In a moment the firing commenced.

The mountain guerillas compensated, for their military indiscipline, by the insuperable energy and perseverance of their character. If they were unable to attack us in the plains—if they failed in combined attacks—they fought most advantageously among the rocks, behind the walls of their houses, and in all places where cavalry could not be used. Montejaque, a little hamlet of fifty or sixty houses, about half a league distant from Ronda, could never be reduced to absolute submission.

The inhabitants of every little town or village among the mountains who expected visits from the French, sent their old people, their wives and their children, to the inaccessible hills, and hid their most precious possessions in caves. The men alone remained to defend the villages, or to make plundering excursions into the plains, to carry off the cattle of those Spaniards who would not declare themselves our foes.

The town of Grazalema was the arsenal of the Serranos. Marshal Soult marched against it with a strong force of three thousand men. The smugglers defended themselves from house to house, and did not abandon the place till their ammunition failed. They then escaped to the mountains, after they had made our soldiers sustain considerable loss. The reoccupied the town again as soon as our force was gone.

A division of three regiments of infantry, sent a month afterwards to disperse the insurgent army anew, easily drove them before them in the open country, but could not expel them from Grazalema. Some of the smugglers were intrenched in the square in the centre of the town, and had placed mattresses before the windows of the houses where they had taken refuge. Twelve Hussars of the tenth regiment, and forty voltigeurs, who formed the vanguard of the French division, arrived there without meeting any resistance. But they never returned. They were all struck down by a fire from the windows, discharged on them all at once. Those who were sent after them to take possession of the square, perished in the same way, without injuring one of their foes. The frequent expeditions we sent among the high mountains, almost always dispersed the enemy, without reducing them; but our troops returned to Ronda much fewer than when they went.

The Serranos, by their system of fighting, frustrated our troops, even though they were superior in numbers. They moved from rock to rock, and from one position to another at the approach of our soldiers, without ever needing to cease their damaging fire. Even as they fled, they destroyed whole columns, without affording one opportunity of revenge. This mode of fighting had procured for them the name of "Mountain Flies," even from the Spaniards; in allusion to the way in which these restless guerillas—like insects torment mankind—harried our army ceaslessly without allowing them any respite.

Every detachment that went out of Ronda either for reconnoitring or otherwise, was attacked by sharpshooters, from the moment of its departure to its return. Every convoy of provisions we brought in cost us several lives. We might have truly said in Scriptural language, that we "ate our own flesh, and drank our own blood," in this inglorious war. It was an like an atonement for the injustice of the cause in which we fought.

The mountains of the kingdoms of Grenada and Murcia were no more submissive than those of Ronda. The French troops, attacked by the whole population of the country at every point, were in almost parallel circumstances with our regiment, in every mountainous district of the Peninsula. Such is a specimen of the repose we enjoyed, after Spain had been conquered, from the frontiers of France to the gates of Cadiz. The siege of that city was now the only military affair of any importance.

When our horses had consumed all the fodder of the farms around Ronda, we were obliged to go farther off, and to send parties of thirty or forty Hussars, three or four times a week, for straw, several leagues from the city. The weakness of the garrison did not permit us to support our cavalry foragers with detachments of foot, eeven though such support was very necessary. Our horsemen were not always sufficiently strong to repulse the enemy in these petty expeditions, and we attempted to elude their vigilance by taking a different road every day, or making a great circuit to avoid the dangerous glens. Not infrequently we were obliged to make a path for ourselves through the heart of the insurgents, who always surrounded the city.

For a month my fortune had been most successful. I succeeded in every enterprise with which I was charged; and the days that I commanded the main guard, none of the soldiers were killed. The Hussars, who are, to a certain extent, fatalists, began to think me invulnerable. On the 1st of May, however, I was seriously wounded. But I have been since told, as a consolation, that Fate made a mistake, that I ought not to think myself less fortunate than formerly, for the adjutant-major had erred in ordering the service, and I went in the place of a comrade who had very bad luck.

On the 1st of May I accompanied a detachment of forty-five Hussars, under the command of a captain. We were going to seek for straw, four leagues from Ronda in the farms around the village of Settenil. A hundred peasants and muleteers from the town attended us, to take charge of the asses and mules. We set off at 5 a. m., and the captain and I rode at the head. In passing a defile, about half a league out, we observed to each other, that surely the enemy must have heard nothing of our excursion, or they would have been watching us here. They could have done us much damage without running any risk themselves. On ascending a steep hill, I first of all spotted, a good way off, a cloud of dust; and then distinctly on our right, about four or five hundred armed men, who were advancing in the valley toward the village of Ariate. I told the captain that I had seen the enemy, and that I was sure of it was they from their hurried and disorderly way of marching.

A quartermaster declared that the men observed in the plain were muleteers returning to Ossuna from Ronda, where they had gone the previous day, with biscuits and cartridges, and an escort of two hundred men. I stoutly maintained that those I saw were enemies; and added, that if I had the command I would charge them instantly whilst they were still in the plain. "If we are repulsed here," I said, "we could easily retreat, but we cannot complete our journey, without being exposed on our return to an attack in some pass unfavourable for cavalry." The captain was of a different opinion; and we continued our route, and soon came near the village of Settenil.

The laziness and surliness of our mule drivers aroused our suspicion. We had still more reason to be alarmed, when, just as we were preparing to return to Ronda, we saw a peasant on horseback on a distant hill observing our march, and then galloping off as if to inform the enemy.

When we had done foraging, we returned the same way we came. A convoy of mules was made to pass on before us, between a vanguard of twelve Hussars and the body of the troop, at whose head rode the captain and myself. When within two gun-shots of the pass we had most reason to fear, I saw a man on the top of an olive-tree, cutting branches from it with a hatchet. I rode forward at the gallop, and asked him if he had seen the Serranos. He was one himself, as I afterwards learned, and was cutting down the branches to interrupt our passage. He replied, pretending to redouble his activity, that "he was too busy to attend to what was passing around him." At the same instant the captain also interrogated a child, five or six years old, who, with a hesitating low voice, as if afraid of being heard, gave him some confused and contradictory answer. To this we gave little heed; for we just then saw our vanguard and the foremost of the convoy emerge from the far side of the glen, and ascend the opposite hill. We had a very narrow and slippery piece of road to pass, bounded on the sides by high garden hedges, and about five or six hundred paces long. Here we were obliged to march in file. The captain made the same observation to me he did in the morning, that it was a fortunate thing for us the enemy had not stationed an ambuscade in this pass. Scarcely had he said these words, when a volley of four or five shots from behind the hedges killed the three last mules of the convoy, and the trumpeters horse before us. That instant our horses stopped.

The captain should have been the first to proceed, but the animal he rode had belonged to a dead officer, killed on a like occasion a few days previously, and it would not move a step. Seeing this, I applied the spurs, and sprung past the captain; I leaped over the trumpeter's horse, and also the mules and their burdens that had just fallen, and passed through the defile alone. The Serranos, concealed behind the hedges, imagined that I was followed closely by the whole troop, and all their muskets were in a moment discharged. I was struck by two of the balls. The one passed through my left thigh; the other entered my body.

The captain followed not far behind, and arrived at the end of the pass unhurt. Of the whole detachment, no more than four of the last were killed; for the enemy required a few minutes to reload their guns, and make a second discharge. The quartermaster, who brought up the rear, had his horse killed; but he counterfeited death, crept into the brushwood, and at midnight returned to Ronda as well as ever.

When we had rallied, and formed in battle-order on the other side of the glen, I told the captain that I was wounded, that I felt my strength exhausted, and that I would return to Ronda by the nearest road, though it was very steep. He recommended that I stay with the troop, which was going to make a compass of half a league round the margin of the plain, where no enemy need be feared, so that it was not exposed to a second attack unnecessarily. I felt that I could not undertake so long a march, and entered the hilly road with a Hussar escorting me, to hold my horse's bridle. As I was losing much blood, I was obliged to summon up all my firmness, lest I should faint. If I had fallen from my horse, the poniard would doubtless have ended my days. I held by the pommel of the saddle with my hands, and made vain efforts to spur my horse forward with the only leg I could use. The poor animal could go no faster, but staggered at every step he took, for a ball had shot him through.

When I was about half a league from the city, my horse could scarcely move. The Hussar who attended me, rode off at the gallop, to tell the picquet on the top of the hill. I made a few paces by myself, without seeing anything, and scarcely even hearing the shots fired at me by some peasants cutting down wood a little way off. The soldiers at length arrived to aid me, and I was carried to my lodgings in my horse-blanket.

I was met by my Spanish hosts, who would not let me be taken to the military hospital, where an epidemic fever raged. I would in all probability have found death for a cure there, as had many others. My hosts had, to that day, treated me with a cold and distant politeness, regarding me as an enemy of their country. This feeling of patriotism, which I respected, had made me as reserved towards them. But when I was wounded, they displayed the most tender concern for my welfare, and treated me with that generosity and kindness which so eminently characterize the Spaniards. They said to me, that since I could do no more harm to Spain, they considered me as a member of their family. Without leaving me a moment for fifty days, they indeed rendered me all the attention which human nature could have showed.

At daybreak on the 4th of May, the insurgents came

to attack Ronda in greater strength than they had ever before mustered. The bells passed so near the windows of my room, that my guardians found it necessary to remove my bed to the adjoining chamber. My host and hostess soon after came to tell me, but with an air of calmness they struggled to preserve, that the guerillas were at the end of the street, that they were fast gaining ground, and that the old city was on the point of falling into their hands. They declared that they would use every effort to save me from the fury of the Serranos, until General Valdenebro, who was their relation, should arrive. They accordingly hastily concealed my arms, my military dress, and every thing else which could have betrayed me to the enemy. With the assistance of their servants, they bore me to the top of the house, behind a little chapel, dedicated to the Virgin Mary, considering that consecrated spot as an asylum secure from trespass. My hosts then hastened to get two priests, whom they stationed before the street-door to guard the entrance in case of danger, and to defend me by their very presence.

An old lady, the mother of my hostess, remained alone with me engaged in prayer. As the shouts of the combatants, and the noise of firearms, announced that the tide of battle advanced and retreated, so did she count the beads of her rosary faster or slower. About noon the firing became fainter, and then ceased altogether. The enemy were beaten in every quarter, and my comrades came to give me an acount of the engagement as soon as they were able.

The Second Hussars received orders a few days after to go to Santa Maria. They were replaced by the forty-third regiment of the line; and of all my corps, none but myself remained at Ronda. I knew none of the officers of the new garrison, and no other Frenchman visited me but a subaltern adjutant of infantry, who came from time to time to inquire of my hosts if I was dead yet, or gone. He was very impatient to obtain possession of my quarters.

After my comrades were gone, my hosts redoubled their care and kindness towards me. They spent several hours of the day in my chamber; and when I became convalescent, they invited some of their neighbours every evening to chat at my bedside, and perform a little concert to divert my mind from its sorrows., They sung their national airs, and accompanied them on the guitar.

My hostess's mother had conceived a great friendship for me, ever since the day she prayed so fervently for my deliverance when the city was assaulted. Her second daughter was a nun in a convent for noble ladies, and she now and then inquired after me, and sent little baskets of perfumed lint covered with rose leaves. The nuns of the different convents of Ronda fasted and did penance more often after we entered Andalusia, than before. They passed the greater part of the night praying for success for the Spanish cause, and the day was spent in preparing medicaments to send to the wounded French. This incongruous mixture of patriotism and Christian charity was by no means rare in Spain.

On the 18th of June, I rose for the first time since I was wounded. I was obliged to begin my sad apprenticeship of walking with crutches, having totally lost the use of one of my legs. I went to see the horse that had been wounded along with me. He had become quite recovered, but did not know me at first, which showed how much I must have changed by my experience. I left Ronda on the 22nd, on an ammunition-waggon, which was going to Ossuna under a strong escort for cartridges. I bade adieu to my hosts with the same kind of grief as is felt on leaving, for the first time, the paternal roof. They were no less sad at my departure, for the kindness which I had experienced at their hands, had made them love me as their own.

I went from Ossuna to Essica, and from thence to Cordova. Bands of Spanish partisans, two or three hundred strong, scoured the country in all directions. When pursued, they retreated to the mountains which separated Andalusia from La Mancha and Estremadura, or to mountains close to the sea. These numerous guerilla bodies worked to keep up that universal state of agitation which prevailed throughout the country; and they also maintained communications between Cadiz and the interior of Spain. They told the people such stories, as that the Marquis de la Romana had beaten the French at Truxillo, or that the English from Gibraltar had completely defeated the French near the shore. These reports, most industriously scattered, though quite improbable, were always received with delight. Hope, thus continually kept alive, stirred up the nation, in one part or other, to partial revolts, and the news of success against us, no matter how spurious, often preceded reports that were true.

At a little distance from Cordova, there existed a most noted band of robbers. These thieves by profession, never abandoned the practice of plundering Spanish passengers. But by way of discharging the obligation which every subject contracts at his birth, of shedding his blood for his country when invaded by foreign foes, these brigands also lifted arms against the French, and attacked their detachments when they could, though they had no prospect of gain.

After leaving Andalusia, I travelled across La Mancha. I was obliged to stop several days at each French outpost, waiting for the return of the escorts that regularly conveyed ammunition to the siege of Cadiz. Sometimes completely wearied out by staying long in such wretched lodgings, I have abandoned myself to my fate, and ventured to go un-accompanied from one place to another. The command-ers at the different communication posts could not spare a convoy but for the essential service of the army, for they often lost several soldiers when escorting a single courier a few leagues.

King Joseph could not devise a plan for collecting his revenues regularly. It was to no purpose that he troops to scour the country. The people fled to the mountains, or, with more courage, defended themselves in their houses. The soldiers pillaged the villages, and the contributions were not received. Peaceable inhabitants sometimes had to pay for all the rest, but were again more heavily oppressed by the guerrilla chiefs, because they had not fled at the approach of the French. The inhabitants of La Mancha, as well as those of other provinces adjoining, were exas-perated by all these grievances which they blamed on us, and the number of our enemies increased every day. New Castile, which I passed through also in my journey, was not more tranquil than the province of La Mancha. The Spanish partisans were at the point of taking King Joseph prisoner in one of his own country-houses near Madrid; and often the French were carried off before the gates, and sometimes from the very streets of the capital.

I stayed almost a month at Madrid, waiting for an op-portunity to depart. It was an easy matter to get there from Bayonne, because numerous detachments were always go-ing from thence to reinforce the armies in Spain. But to get permission to return to France, it was necessary to be lame. The Board of Health received the strictest orders; and they granted no leave but to those wounded officers or soldiers of whom they had not the slightest hope of recovery. I was numbered with those who had thus a right to return. Even at the price I paid, I was glad to be out of a war so lacking in glory and unjust; in my soul I never ceased to disapprove of the acts which my hands were compelled to commit.

I left Madrid with a numerous caravan of invalid officers, who were going to France under an escort of only seventy-five foot-soldiers.

We were a platoon of cripples, commanded by the senior wounded, that we might die in arms if attacked. We were incapable of defending ourselves; and many of us had to be tied on horseback, to enable us to keep our seats.

Two of our company were insane. The first was a Hussar, who had lost his reason due to severe wounds he had received on the head. He marched on foot, having been deprived of his horse and his arms, for fear of his escaping or doing mischief. Notwithstanding his derangement, he had not forgotten his degree of rank, and the name of his regiment. Sometimes he took off his hat before us, and showed us the scars of real wounds, which he pretended to have gotten in imaginary battles, of which he spoke incessantly. Our convoy being one day attacked on the march, he eluded his keepers, and recovered his former intrepidity for thrashing enemies, armed with nothing but a simple stick. He called this cane "the magic sceptre of the Grand Sultan of Morocco".

The other was an old Flemish musician of Light Infantry, whose brain the warmth of Spanish wine had inspired for life with an unmoveable gaiety. He had exchanged his clarinet for a fiddle, which he used to play at the entertainments of his native village when a boy. He marched in the middle of our melancholy troop, both playing and dancing without cease.

Not one solitary traveller appeared on the long lonely road we journied; only, we met every two or three days convoys of ammunition, or other escorts, who lodged with us under the shelter of crumbling huts, whose windows and doors had been carried off to supply the French armies with wood. Instead of that crowd of children and idlers that flock, in time of peace, to meet strangers at the entrance of villages, we perceived a small post of French issuing from behind palisades and barriers, calling to us to "halt," that they might know who we were. Sometimes, too, a sentinel would unexpectedly appear, stationed on some old tower in a deserted village—like a solitary owl among ruins.

The nearer we approached France, the more our danger from the partisans increased. At every outpost we found detachments from different parts of the Peninsula, waiting our arrival to go with us. Whole battalions—whole regiments, reduced to mere skeletons, or to a very few men—sadly returned with their eagles and colours, to recruit in France, Italy, Switzerland, Germany, and Poland. Our convoy left Spain at the end of July, twenty days after Ciudad Rodrigo, a strong fortress of the province of Salamanca, had fallen to our army.

Chapter 9

THE CAMPAIGN IN PORTUGAL

Here I ought to close these Memoirs; because, having left Spain at this period of the war, I have not witnessed what followed with my own eyes. But since then, during a year's residence in England, I have collected materials which could not, at the time, be procured on the Continent; and am, therefore, enabled to add to my narrative that of the Campaign of Portugal—the masterpiece both of national and military defence.

After the campaign of Austria, and the peace concluded at Vienna in 1809, France saw herself free from all her Northern wars; and the whole of Europe believed, that once again would Spain and Portugal fall under the power of the mighty armies that the Emperor Napoleon could raise. That conqueror had announced, that he would chase the English from the Peninsula; and that, in one year, the world would witness his triumphal eagles planted on the forts of Lisbon. He forthwith sent powerful supplies to Spain, for the purpose of invading Portugal.

The French army destined for that invasion, was more than 80,000 strong. The Commander-in-chief was Marshal Massena; and it was divided into three divisions, under the orders of Marshals Ney, Junot, and Reynier. The first two of these corps united in the neighbourhood of Salamanca, and occupied the country between the rivers

Douro and Tagus. The third, that of General Reynier, was in Estremadura, opposite the frontier of Alentejo; its right communicating, at Alcantara, with the left of the corps of Marshal Ney. A fourth corps of reserve assembled at Valladolid, under the command of General Drouet, to reinforce and support the invading army if required.

The army of Lord Wellington, opposed to that of Marshal Massena, counted 30,000 English, and as many Portuguese in its ranks. The Regency of Portugal had, besides that, 15,000 regular troops under arms—several flying corps of Portuguese militia, led by chiefs of their own nation, or by English officers—and levies *en masse*, known by the name of Ordenanzas, which the English estimated only at 45,000, but in fact consisted, in a case of invasion, of the whole armed population of Portugal. They were united against the French by patriotism, hatred, vengeance, and the memory of recent evils they had endured for the two preceding years, during the expeditions of Marshals Junot and Soult—all unsuccessful though they had been.

The indisciplined native bands did incalculable mischief to the French when they fought for their homes, in the gorges of their mountains, where their numbers and local knowledge gave them a great advantage. But beyond their own country they were useless. It was for this reason that the Anglo-Portuguese regular army of Lord Wellington would not move a step from the line of defence it occupied on the frontiers of Portugal, and north and south of the Tagus, notwithstanding all the provocations of the French. The English general was besides afraid to give battle in the plains of the province of Salamanca, where his enemies presented a numerous and formidable body of cavalry.

After the taking of Ciudad Rodrigo, the French passed

the Coa, repulsed the English outposts, invested Almeida on the frontiers of Portugal, and on the 27th of August gained possession of it when it surrendered, thirteen days after the trenches were opened.

General Reynier's corps left Spanish Estremadura, crossed the Tagus at Alcantara, and concentrated itself in the neighbourhood of Almeida, with the two other French divisions. The English corps opposed to that of General Reynier towards Elvas and Portalègre, crossed the Tagus also by a simultaneous movement at Villa-Velha; and the whole army of Lord Wellington retreated by the left bank of the Mondego, to the impregnable position of the Sierra de Murcella behind the Alva.

The French army left the environs of Almeida on the 15th of September, entered the valley watered by the river Mondego the day following, passed that river at Celorico, and again repassed it at the bridge of Fornos. Marshal Massena led his army along the right bank of the Mondego, intending by a rapid movement to seize on Coimbra, which he believed the English had left quite exposed when retiring by the opposite bank.

The French arrived at Vizeu on the 21st, where they were obliged to halt two whole days waiting for their artillery, whose arrival had been delayed by the poor roads, and the attacks of the Portuguese militia. On the 24th their vanguard discovered the English picquets stationed on the opposite bank of the river Dao, and beat them back after repairing the bridges which had been broken down. Lord Wellington had made his army hastily cross from the left to the right bank of the Mondego, in order to defend the defiles of the mountains on the way to Coimbra. He had left but a single brigade of infantry and a force of cavalry, in his former position of Sierra de Murcella.

On the 25th and 26th, the French corps arrived successively at the foot of the mountains Sierra de Busaco, whose summits they found occupied by the Anglo-Portuguese army. At six oclock, on the morning of the 27th, they marched in column against the right and centre of that army, in the two roads leading to Coimbra, by the village of San Antonio de Cantaro, and by the convent of Busaco. These roads were cut up in several places, and defended by artillery. The mountain over which they pass is surrounded with steep rocks, and is very difficult to access.

The French column which attacked the right of the English advanced with intrepidity, in spite of the fire of the English artillery and light troops. It reached the top of the hill after sustaining considerable loss, and began to deploy in line with the greatest coolness, and most perfect regularity. But a superior force again assaulted it, and compelled it to retire. It soon rallied, made a second attack, and was again repulsed. The French battalions, which advanced against the convent of Busaco, where the left and centre of the English army joined, were also driven back, a little before they reached that post. General Simon, who had been struck by two balls during the charge, was left on the height, and a great many wounded officers and soldiers.

The position occupied by the English and Portuguese on the brow of the hill, formed the arc of a circle, whose two extremes enclosed the ground over which the French had to advance. The allied army saw the least movements made below them, and had time to form to receive any powerful force before it arrived. This circumstance materially contributed to the advantage they obtained. The French lost 1,800 men in their attacks, and had nearly 3,000 wounded. The English and Portuguese had no more than 1,235 of their army disabled from fighting.

Marshal Massena judged that the position of Lord Wellington could not be carried in front, and resolved to turn it. He kept up an irregular fire till the evening, and sent off a body of troops by the mountain road, which leads from Mortago to Oporto. The English and Portuguese, in consequence of this movement, abandoned their position on the mountain of Busaco.

The French entered Coimbra on the 1st of October, continued their route, and on the 12th, after eleven days of forced marches under heavy rains, they arrived at Alenquer, nine leages distant from Lisbon. They had almost reached the farthest extremity of Portugal, and already regarded that country as their undoubted prize. They believed that the English would think of nothing else but embarking— they calculated on reaching them next day, obliging them to fight in the hurry of departure, and crushing them by a superior force.

But some reconnoitring parties, despatched in different directions, discovered Lord Wellington's army intrenched in a position between the sea and the Tagus, on the chain of mountains which stretch from Alhandra to Torres Vedras, and to the mouth of the Sisandro towards Mafra, in the rear. This position is so advantageous that it could neither be attacked nor turned.

Passes, naturally strong, bristled here and there with most powerful artillery. Art had vied with Nature in erecting defences where death could be inflicted, without sustaining any harm in return. Throughout the whole breadth of the advanced part of the Peninsula in which Lisbon is situated, as if it had been all one fortified city, there reigned in all the posts of the English and Portuguese the greatest silence, calmness, and good order. Sloops of war on the Tagus flanked the right of their position; and a ball from one of their cannon killed, on our first day there, General Saint Croix, who had gone forward to the top of a hill to make some observations.

The French tried, by every provocation, to induce Lord Wellington to give battle; but it was all in vain. That modern Fabius remained immoveable in his lines, and contemplated from his high rocks his enemies underneath with admirable unconcern. Wisely economical of the blood of his men, he refused to spill it for his personal ambition, or to risk, by one battle, the fate of the country he was intrusted to defend. It was to the vengeance of the natives that he wished to leave the French. He pursued a plan most deeply calculated, in suffering them to perish with hunger and disease—the never-failing scourges of invading armies, when they are not welcomed and seconded by the nations wishes.

At the call of Lord Wellington, and the command of the Regency of Portugal, the entire population of the valley of Mondego, and part of that of the north bank of the Tagus, left their dwellings in a body. All the able bodied men had previously retired to the mountains with their cattle and their arms; and at the approach of the French, there remained only an immense crowd of old men, women, children, priests and nuns, who simultaneously destroyed their own means of subsistence, to put them out of their enemies reach, and then retired to Lisbon to be under the protection of the English army.

The benevolence of several convents, stirred up by patriotism, and seconded by liberal alms, at first supplied the wants of these voluntary exiles, who, to save their country, had resigned themselves to Providence. In the streets, in the squares, and without the walls of Lisbon, a peaceful camp was formed for them behind the English fortifications, which was nearly as essential to the prosperity of Portugal, as the armed warriors who struggled in her cause.

The French, in their rapid march between Almeida and Alenquer, by their own admission, found only deserted towns and villages, mills made useless, wine flowing in the streets, corn burned to ashes, and even furniture broken to pieces. They saw neither horse, mule, ass, cow, nor goat. They were obliged to subsist on their own beasts of burden, and the limited supply of biscuit they brought along with them to Portugal; for they calculated on obtaining by conquest the vast resources of one of the wealthiest capitals in Europe.

Unexpectedly stopped, when they fancied themselves on the eve of terminating their travels, they were compelled to live on the victuals which the soldiers individually procured. Chance, necessity, native cunning, and the long habit of a wandering, warring life, enabled them sometimes to discover provisions in the secret places where the natives had buried them, to be out of their enemies reach.

On every side the French were surrounded, and their communications were all intercepted by the raiding parties of the enemy, even before they reached the lines of Torres Vedras. Coimbra, where a garrison had been left, and also sick and wounded to the number of five thousand, was retaken by the Portuguese militia on the 7th, together with other French posts on the right bank of the Mondego river. The roads by which the army of Massena should have received their provisions and ammunition, had all been occupied by the Portuguese troops, commanded by Generals Silveira and Bacellar, and the militia of Colonels Trant, Miller, Wilson, and Grant. The right flank of his army was also harassed by frequent sorties from the garrisons of Peniche, Ourem, and of Obidos. The peasant bands and the militia corps, united to attack the detachments and foraging parties of the French, whose daily bread was obtained at the cost of many lives.

While these individual contests raged in their rear, and on their flanks, with all the zeal that vengeance and national hatred could inspire, the English, always on the watch within their lines, enjoyed the most perfect peace, and lost not a single man. Their videttes never fired on those of the French; and their advanced posts did not attempt, by false attacks, to provoke or vex each other. This profound tranquillity which reigned between the two armies, was the result of that kind of tacit convention which usually exists between regular armies, who, though antagonists, have neither hatred nor passion to gratify, because they are only indirectly interested in the cause for which they are fighting.

The French continued waiting below the lines of Torres Vedras, suffering the many privations with patience, in the hope that they would shortly reduce their enemies to despair. They trusted that the immense crowd of people, of every description, which they had driven before them, and shut up with the inhabitants of the capital in a narrow infertile spot, would starve their enemys army, and compel them to fight or to re-embark. But the English and Portuguese had the broad ocean behind them; and their swift and numerous ships had freedom to bring supplies from anywhere. Provisions, at first, were supplied from England and Brazil; and, afterwards, numerous trading vessels, allured by the prospect of gain, brought to the Tagus the abundance of Africa and America, and the nearer supplies of the provinces in Spain and Portugal that had not been invaded by our army.

The French, weakened by daily losses, and by sickness, the lack of supplies and inactivity began, at length, to find them in the very situation to which they had hopes to reduce their foes.

Their detachments were kept from foraging in their rear, towards Upper Estremadura, by the river Zezere, and the town of Abrantes. The bridges of the Tagus, on their left, being destroyed, they were separated, by this means, from Lower Estremadura and Alentejo. These districts had hitherto been untouched; and their proximity tended to increase the desire which the French, amid their distresses, naturally had to possess them. They made several unsuccessful attempts to force the passage of the Tagus, in order to get at these much wished for provinces. Among others, they threatened the inhabitants of Chamusca, a small village on the opposite bank, that, if they did not bring over their boats, they would set fire to their dwellings. The fishermen, to whom the boats belonged, put an end to the question, by burning them all immediately. The country then flew to arms; and the English made large numbers of infantry and cavalry cross the Tagus to frustrate the plans of the French. Lord Wellington had received a reinforcement of 10,000 Spaniards, brought by the Marquis de la Romana; and by employing, in the land service, some cannoneers of the English fleet, he was enabled to despatch these divisions to guard the opposite banks, without weakening his lines.

The French having now waited below the lines of Torres Vedras for more than a month between Villa Franca, Sobral, Villa Nueva, Otta and Aleventre, began to find themselves in absolute starvation. They broke up their camp during the night of the 14th of November, and retreated to take up a position at Santarem, behind the Rio Major. The order and silence of their departure was such, that the English videttes opposite those of the French, were not aware till daybreak that their enemies had withdrawn.

The English, afraid that this movement of the French was intended to force the passage of the Tagus, sent over considerable reinforcements to strengthen the troops that were already there. Their army left the lines they had occupied on the 19th, and, following the route of the French, advanced in fighting columns opposite Santarem, near to the Rio Major, apparently determined to force the passage of that river. But they renounced this design when they saw the strength of the French position. Lord Wellington established his headquarters at Cartaxo, placing his advanced posts on the right bank of the Rio Major, between that river and his former lines, that he might be ready to return there again if the French would come back and attack him with a superior force.

Santarem is situated on the summit of a lofty and almost perpendicular chain of mountains. In front of them is a range of hills, on which the first of the French lines was extended. The Rio Major runs at the foot of these heights, and a little farther off flows the Tagus. The English had to cross a large extent of marshy ground by two causeways, which, as well as the bridge, were completely commanded by artillery.

Marshal Massena had wisely chosen and fortified the position of Santarem, with the view of keeping the English in check on the Rio Major with very few troops, and of enabling him without any risk to extend his cantonments to the river Zezere, over which he caused two bridges to be thrown. He occupied both its banks with infantry, in order to overawe Abrantes, and protect the detachments sent to forage in Upper Estremadura. He wished to establish communications with Spain by the route of Thomar, until the reinforcemeuts for which he looked, and that were indispensable to the continuance of his operations after the losses he had sustained, should arrive, and chase the Portuguese militia from the posts on the roads in the valley of Mondego, which had all been seized.

The *corps-de-reserve* under General Drouet, had left Valladolid on the 12th of October, on its way to the Portuguese frontier. The division of General Gardanne, which had remained to garrison Ciudad Rodrigo and Almeida, had also commenced its march, to rejoin the army of Massena; but on the 14th of November, it had suddenly fallen back towards the Spanish territory, after approaching to within a few leagues of the first French posts. These forces were deceived regarding the situation by the great number of Portuguese militia, which had never ceased to harass it since it crossed their frontiers, and had even destroyed its vanguard. General Gardanne joined with the troops of General Drouet, and again entered Portugal in the month of December.

The corps of General Drouet took its route by the valley of Mondego, and joined the army of Marshal Massena, after dispersing the hostile militia, but, as usual, not destroying them. The Portuguese General Silveira returned at the end of the month to attack the division of Claparède, who had been left at Trancoso and Pinhel, in the district of Coa, to preserve the communications of the army in Portugal with Spain. General Claparède united his division in consequence, routed General Silveira, and pursued him to the Douro. But he was obliged to retrace his steps to Trancoso and Guarda, on account of the movements of other bodies of militia under General Bacellar and Colonel Wilson, who, on the Pavio and at Castro Diaro, attacked his flanks and his rear.

These corps of militia never ventured to attack any but the weak parts of the army, such as the rear and vanguards, detachments, petty garrisons, or isolated troops, to whom they did incalculable mischief; and their numbers and local knowledge rendered it impossible that they could be destroyed. If they were dispersed in one place, they rallied in another, and everywhere, united with them in their expeditions, the armed population of the country.

General Drouet arrived at Leyria, and with the other

French corps occupied the country between the sea and the Tagus, towards Punhète and Santarem. Marshal Massena caused a number of boats to be built at Punhète, in order to throw a bridge across the Tagus; a serious undertaking in a country depopulated of its inhabitants, and which affords but limited resources at best. The English corps who occupied Mugem, Almerin, Chamusca, and Saint Brito, on the opposite bank, observed these preparations, and, to oppose them, began to construct batteries of very considerable strength.

It was of as much importance to the English to prevent the crossing of this river, as it was to the French to achieve it. The fate of Portugal, and the success of the future operations of either party, appeared at the time to depend on this one maneuvre. If Marshal Massena succeeded in his design, the English would be obliged to divide their force, and greatly to weaken themselves, by extending their lines on both sides of the river. The positions of Torres Vedras being less ably guarded, and being deprived of many necessary defenders, might then have been carried at the cost of many lives, by a French corps advancing from Lena upon Lisbon. If, on the other hand, the English had concentrated their troops within the lines of Torres Vedras, the French might have descended in the direction of the Tagus, after crossing it, and seized the small peninsula on which are built the towns of Palmela and Setubal. From its extremity, they might have commanded the course of the Tagus, and starved the city of Lisbon. From the heights of Almada opposite, they might have bombarded this capital city.

On the 9th of January, Marshals Soult and Mortier arrived at Merida with all the available forces of the army of Andalusia, planning to lay siege to Badajoz and Elvas, and of thus cooperating with Marshal Massena, by obliging Lord Wellington to divide his army in defending that part of the Portuguese frontier. On the news of their approach toward Alentejo, the English sent additional troops under Generals Hill and Beresford to the south of the Tagus; and the inhabitants thereabout prepared to lay waste to the countryside, that the French might be famished, according to the defensive system so successfully pursued by Lord Wellington on the left bank of the river.

To support Badajoz, General Mendizabal was sent by the Marquis de Ia Romana with the 10,000 Spaniards he had brought to the lines of Torres Vedras. The Marquis was then sick with the illness from which he died on the 24th of January at Cartaxo. He was deeply missed by the English and Spaniards, and died with the esteem of his enemies, because he had never despaired of his country's cause, but persevered in continuing the war, amid endless disappointments, with such activity and resolution as usually belong only to conquerors. Marshals Soult and Mortier took Olivenza on the 23rd of January, and on the 19th of February they crossed the Gevora and the Guadiana, invaded Badajoz, and surprised and cut to pieces in his camp, the Spanish General Mendizabal and his army.

By this time the army of Marshal Massena had exhausted all the provisions which could be procured on the right bank of the Tagus; and his foragers were obliged to extend their excursions to a circuit of twenty leagues. A great part of the army had to be continually occupied in providing for the wants of the remainder; and sufficient food was daily obtained only by very grievous losses. Marshal Junot having learned that the English had formed a store of wine and corn on the Rio Major, went with two regiments of cavalry, and some infantry of his own corps, to appropriate it to the French. The English retired in time, and the Marshal was wounded in a slight skirmish, which happened between his advanced guard and the rear of the enemy.

Cavalry ought, in a manner, to be the eyes and arms of a powerful army, being designed to procure and guard their provisions; but they were a burden to the French by their very numbers, and the difficulty of providing them with food. Besides, they were often useless in a mountainous country; intersected with defiles, and constantly infested with armed swarms of peasantry and militia.

The rage and hatred of the invaded nation, increased with the continuance of the war, because of the hardships they endured. The most timid peasants, who had fled to the mountains only for the sake of peace, were driven, by hunger and despair, from their otherwise undisturbed retreats. They poured down into the valleys, lay in ambush near the roads, and hung about the French in the difficult passes, to snatch back from them the very victuals of which they had been previously plundered themselves. A peasant, in the vicinity of Thomar, chose a cavern near that town as his place of refuge. During the month of February, he killed with his own hand more than thirty Frenchmen, whom he surprised separately; and carried off about fifty horses and mules.

Since so great a proportion of our force had been employed in Portugal, the guerrillas of Spain had become bolder than ever. Spanish chiefs who had not more than a few hundreds under them seven months before, now found themselves commanding formidable numbers, that frequently seized the convoys of ammunition and arms, destined for our armies in Portugal. Before these convoys could reach their destination, they had to cross a tract of hostile territory near two hundred leagues in extent. They were composed of muleteers, sent from the south of France; and Spanish peasants, who were forced to aid us, and were thus in danger of retribution from their countrymen. These peasants fled at the first opportunity that offered itself, or sent notice beforehand to the guerrillas, so that when attacked they might not be killed. The least negligence on the part of these escorts, would have deprived the whole army of food.

By the beginning of March, Marshal Massena had finished the building of two hundred boats, and all his preparations for crossing the Tagus were completed. But he dared not attempt the passage without additional reinforcements. Marshals Soult and Mortier could render him no effectual assistance, by advancing towards the Opposite bank, until Badajoz was destroyed; and this city still held out.

Such was the dearth of supplies that when a convoy of biscuit, expected from France, was taken by the Spanish partisans, on the point of absolute starvation, our forces were obliged to think of a retreat. They abandoned Portugal, after a campaign of seven months, without having fought one regular battle. The English commander made his enemies yield to his perseverance, in pursuing a plan which left no chance of victory to others, by never affording them one opportunity of fighting.

On the 4th of March, the sick, the wounded, and the baggage of the French, departed on an immense train of beasts of burden, and the whole army next day commenced its retreat. Marshal Ney, who was charged with the care of the rear guard, advanced with his corps from Leyria to Muliano, to menace, by this offensive demonstration, the flanks of the English army, and oblige them to remain inactive, whilst the other French corps were making progress.

The French reached Pombal on the 10th, and their rear guard detained for the whole of the 11th, the vanguard of the English before that town. They abandoned it towards night, and moved onward, under cover of darkness, to the strong position of Redinha on the Adanços. They repassed that defile on the approach of the English, under the protection of artillery stationed on the neighbouring heights, which thundered down on the vanguard of their enemies. The French rear formed in order of battle behind the pass of Redinha, and withdrew to the main body, which halted for them in the position of Condeixa.

The genius of the French, says an English writer, was every moment manifest. They suffered no advantage of the ground to pass unimproved. Their rear guards never abandoned a position they were charged to defend, until it was beyond defence, and then they only left it to take up a new position, and to commence a fresh defence. The French columns slowly retired to one central point in a chosen position, where they all united in a body to rest, to face the enemy, to repulse them, and again renew their march. Marshal Ney, with some chosen troops, covered the retreat, whilst Marshal Massena directed the march of the main body, and kept himself always ready to sustain the rear, if it required his help. "Never," says the English Military Journal, "did the talents of this great captain shine so conspicuously; nothing can equal the skill he then displayed."

The French took up their position on the Ceira during the 15th, leaving a force at the village of Foz de Aronce, where a pretty brisk engagement happened. On the 16th they broke down the bridge over the Ceira, and left their position on the 17th to retire behind the Alva. There the English army stopped to wait for provisions; and as far as Guarda the French were followed only by light troops, Portuguese militia, and the people of the country they crossed—who with bitter rage incessantly harassed them, and gave no quarter to the wounded or to stragglers who fell into their hands.

Want compelled the French to march fast. In leaving Portugal they found it as they entered. The cities were deserted, the houses were empty, and no provisions could be found. The French soldiers, exasperated by their hardships and privations, gave vent to every kind of atrocity, and some villages and even towns were set on fire. In their rapacious pillage they profaned the churches and despoiled them of their ornaments—they violated the tombs and dispersed the sacred relics—they wreaked their vengeance on the guiltless ashes of the dead, when the living were beyond their reach.

The French remained at Guarda till the 28th, and on the approach of the English, abandoned that town to occupy the strong position of Ruivinha. They defended the ford of Rapoula de Coa on the 3rd with some advantage; and on the 4th they repassed the Portuguese frontier, leaving a small garrison behind them in Almeida.

The defensive system which obliged the army of Massena to abandon Portugal, after having invaded it, was the same as that practised in Spain. Every nation that has a spark of patriotism may employ it with parallel success. It consists of nothing more than just avoiding regular battles, and obliging a powerful army to break itself down into weak disunited corps, for the purpose of carrying on a war in detail. Again, if it remains united, nothing more is necessary than to cripple it, by destroying every means of procuring its supplies, which will be the easier the greater its numbers, and the further removed by its conquests from the country they should become.

In the great military states of central Europe, where the nations care little about the quarrels of their governments, a battle gained, or a tract of country occupied, supplied the French with everything they wanted. Provisions in abundance, horses, arms, and even soldiers, came pouring in upon them; and it might be said of their army, what Virgil says of Fame—*vires acquirit eundo*—it gained by going.

In Spain and Portugal, on the contrary, the strength of the French diminished as they advanced, by the necessity of detaching numerous corps to oppose the scattered peasantry, to procure provisions, and to preserve an extended line of communication. Their army, even when victorious, found itself soon reduced to the situation of the lion in the fable, who tore himself with his own claws, in vainly attempting to get rid of the flies that continually followed and tormented him.

Europe never should forget that Spain, almost single-handed, fought for upwards of five years Napoleon's great army. Victorious in Italy, on the Danube, on the Elbe, and on the Niemen—he had either crushed or united with him the greatest part of Europe. In joining under his banners the conquered with their conquerors, he had converted his enemies into allies armed in his cause. Italians, Poles, Swiss, Dutch, Saxons, Bavarians, and all the warlike nations of the Confederation of the Rhine, mingled in the ranks with Frenchmen, jealous of their glory, and delighting to show in battle that they too were inspired with contempt for death and danger.

The great Powers of the North and East of Europe, who, in spite of their misfortunes, had still strength enough to contend, were struck powerless by the illusion of Napoleons power. He distributed kingdoms throughout Europe to his companions in arms, as he did governments in France to his followers; and the name and authority of King came at last to be regarded as no more than a step of military promotion in his army.

At the commencement of hostilities in 1808, the French had already invaded Portugal, without striking a blow. They occupied Madrid, the very centre of Spain, and took by stratagem different fortresses throughout that kingdom. The best of the Spanish troops were detained in Germany and Portugal, fighting in the same ranks with the French. Those who stayed behind knew not then to distinguish between the orders of the French, and the will of their own monarchs, Charles IV and Ferdinand VII.

In keeping these sovereigns prisoners in France, and appointing his brother King of Spain, Napoleon hoped that a weak and powerless nation, deprived of leaders, would rather have preferred the rule of a stranger, than the scourge of war on the bosom of their country. Napoleon believed, and all Europe with him, that Spain would have yielded without a struggle.

During the five years of the wars continuance, the French had gained ten pitched battles in succession, and seized almost every citadel in the kingdom; but yet they had not reduced a single province to a permanent submission. Spain had been conquered to the gates of Cadiz, as Portugal to those of Lisbon. Even though both these cities had been taken, the fate of the Peninsula would not then have been sealed. Whilst the French were lying under the walls of Lisbon and Cadiz, troops of Spaniards made incursions to the gates of Toulouse, in the very heart of France.

One and the same spirit inspired the whole Spanish nation—love of liberty, and detestation of those strangers who meant to humble their national pride, and make them the slaves of a foreign yoke. It was neither armies nor fortresses that required conquering in Spain, but the single patriotic feeling which inspired all her citizens.

Since these Memoirs were written, we have witnessed in the north of Europe the Muscovite nation, and the Prussian people also, giving proofs of devotion to their country, in many respects similar to that which has done honour to the Peninsula, Russia, Prussia, and Spain, have all been speedily delivered from their common enemy. These events, which have changed the face of Europe, as power-fully demonstrate, as Spain's long and noble contest, that the real strength of States does not so much consist of the number or valour of their armies, as in a spirit of religious, patriotic, or political enthusiasm, strong enough to engage every individual of a nation in the public cause, as intensely as if it were his own.

LEONAUR

ALSO FROM LEONAUR
AVAILABLE IN SOFTCOVER OR HARDCOVER WITH DUST JACKET

CAPTAIN OF THE 95th (Rifles) *by Jonathan Leach*—An officer of Wellington's Sharpshooters during the Peninsular, South of France and Waterloo Campaigns of the Napoleonic Wars.

THE KHAKEE RESSALAH *by Robert Henry Wallace Dunlop*—Service & adventure with the Meerut volunteer horse during the Indian mutiny 1857-1858

BUGLER AND OFFICER OF THE RIFLES *by William Green & Harry Smith* With the 95th (Rifles) during the Peninsular & Waterloo Campaigns of the Napoleonic Wars

BAYONETS, BUGLES AND BONNETS *by James 'Thomas' Todd*—Experiences of hard soldiering with the 71st Foot - the Highland Light Infantry - through many battles of the Napoleonic wars including the Peninsular & Waterloo Campaigns

A NORFOLK SOLDIER IN THE FIRST SIKH WAR *by J W Baldwin*—Experiences of a private of H.M. 9th Regiment of Foot in the battles for the Punjab, India 1845-46

A CAVALRY OFFICER DURING THE SEPOY REVOLT *by A.R.D. Mackenzie*—Experiences with the 3rd Bengal Light Cavalry, the Guides and Sikh Irregular Cavalry from the outbreak to Delhi and Lucknow

THE ADVENTURES OF A LIGHT DRAGOON *by George Farmer & G.R. Gleig*—A cavalryman during the Peninsular & Waterloo Campaigns, in captivity & at the siege of Bhurtpore, India

THE COMPLEAT RIFLEMAN HARRIS *by Benjamin Harris as told to & transcribed by Captain Henry Curling*—The adventures of a soldier of the 95th (Rifles) during the Peninsular Campaign of the Napoleonic Wars

THE RED DRAGOON *by W.J. Adams*—With the 7th Dragoon Guards in the Cape of Good Hope against the Boers & the Kaffir tribes during the 'war of the axe' 1843-48

THE LIFE OF THE REAL BRIGADIER GERARD - Volume 1 - THE YOUNG HUSSAR 1782 - 1807 *by Jean-Baptiste De Marbot*—A French Cavalryman Of the Napoleonic Wars at Marengo, Austerlitz, Jena, Eylau & Friedland

THE LIFE OF THE REAL BRIGADIER GERARD Volume 2 IMPERIAL AIDE-DE-CAMP 1807 - 1811 *by Jean-Baptiste De Marbot*—A French Cavalryman of the Napoleonic Wars at Saragossa, Landshut, Eckmuhl, Ratisbon, Aspern-Essling, Wagram, Busaco & Torres Vedras